"In a broken, hurting world that longs for hope, Michael Youssef has provided a remedy for our souls that is both biblical and practical. Read this and embrace the healing power of God."

—DR. JOSEPH M. STOWELL, president of Moody Bible Institute
and author of *The Trouble with Jesus*

"Michael Youssef is one of the most gifted pastors of our generation. I recommend *The Spirituality That Heals* to all who seek the healing power of Jesus Christ."

—LARRY BURKETT, author of *Nothing to Fear* and chairman
of the board of Crown Financial Ministries

"Michael Youssef does an inspiring job of teaching the remarkable truth about the work of the Holy Spirit. His book will invite you to empty yourself and seek to be filled with God's Spirit."

—NICKY CRUZ, international evangelist and author
of *One Holy Fire* and *Run, Baby, Run*

DIVINE
Discontent

DIVINE
Discontent

PURSUING THE PEACE
YOUR SOUL LONGS FOR

MICHAEL YOUSSEF, PH.D.

WATERBROOK
PRESS

DIVINE DISCONTENT

PUBLISHED BY WATERBROOK PRESS

2375 Telstar Drive, Suite 160

Colorado Springs, Colorado 80920

A division of Random House, Inc.

ISBN 1-57856-556-1

Printed in the United States of America

2004—First Edition

10 9 8 7 6 5 4 3 2 1

To Moore Theological College, Sydney, Australia,
an institution that was used of God in the early 1970s
to change my life and bring me face to face
with the wonderful knowledge of the grace of God.

⌣

Two men in particular tower in their impact on my thinking:
Broughton Knox and Don Robinson.

CONTENTS

WHY DO WE KEEP LOOKING FOR MORE?

Understanding the Nature of Our Discontent

Are you convinced that if things were different, you would be happier and more at peace? Are you finding less fulfillment in the things that consume most of your time and energy? Is there a steady background hum in your life—the dull hum of dissatisfaction?

This deep-seated discontent is not limited to those who are struggling with life's hurts and tragedies. In fact, a sense of dissatisfaction with life is often more pronounced among people who—from all outward appearances—seem to have it made. One's level of success does nothing to minimize the symptoms of discontent. And Christians are not immune. Large numbers of believers are angry with God, disappointed in their church, or troubled by the requirements that Scripture makes on their lives. Their faith seems to be powerless to quiet the hum of discontent. The nagging inner voice insists, *There has to be more. Something is still missing.*

At some point that same voice whispers into everyone's ear. Many people I know resort to acquisition in an attempt to fill the inner void. Others pursue higher and more visible levels of achievement. Some turn to unhealthy relationships to try to find a sense of belonging. And still others fall victim to addiction—drugs, alcohol, sex, or even work—in their pursuit of meaning and satisfaction.

What lies behind this drive to find contentment? Some observers place the blame on materialism. They point out that advertising and the entertainment media have programmed us to be dissatisfied with our station in life. We've been trained to feel inferior, and we're constantly directed to replace our old things with new things. Then we're tempted to pursue still more things that are bigger and better. But I don't believe a desire for more possessions fully explains the universal disease—or disease, if you will—that plagues us.

Others find the cause in history, arguing that baby boomers and those in Generation X never had to struggle through the Depression or a devastating world war, so they never learned what it means to do without. While I don't fully discount this view, neither do I believe that it explains why the wealthiest country on earth is populated with people who are convinced their lives are falling short.

We enjoy more ease and comfort than any nation in history, yet our hunger for contentment continues to drive us. We might be exhausted by the search, but we dare not stop until we find a resting place. There must be a deeper explanation for such a constant, driving force that pushes us to keep looking for more, hoping that someday we will arrive at true contentment.

THE GOAL OF OUR SEARCH

While most people pursue earthly solutions to quiet their restlessness, God's Word makes it clear that our lack of peace and satisfaction in life is a spiritual issue. As we study the Scriptures, we see that the loss of contentment can push us in one of two directions. The search can either lead us down paths cluttered with false promises of fulfillment, or it can bring us to a place of turning, where the journey takes on a redemptive quality. Our search for contentment can ultimately lead us to the heart of God, which is the *only* place where we will find rest, a place of belonging, and ultimate contentment.

While the search for contentment is as current as today's news, it is also as old as humanity. Adam and Eve forfeited their contentment when they disobeyed God and ate from the forbidden tree. They were banished from the garden, which set in motion an ongoing human quest to regain the peace and settledness that had been forfeited. Men and women through the ages have sought an end to this restlessness.

Early in the history of the church, a man named Augustine was driven to find a way to satisfy his many longings. Honored today as one of the greatest theologians the church has ever produced, Augustine was a brilliant but wayward youth who tried to satisfy his restlessness through sexual immorality. Despite the influence of a godly mother, by the age of eighteen he had taken a mistress and fathered a child. He consulted astrologers and dabbled in pagan philosophies while halfheartedly pursuing a teaching career.

Wanderlust eventually drew Augustine from his home in northern Africa to Milan, where he developed a close friendship with Ambrose, bishop of the church there. With the influence of Ambrose, and through the fervent prayers of his devout mother, Augustine finally embraced the Christian faith. Yet he still struggled with sexual temptation. At his mother's insistence, Augustine sent away his mistress, but he soon fell into the arms of another woman.

How Augustine overcame his lustful pursuits and found peace is recounted in his memoir, *Confessions,* written in A.D. 400. He finally came to a moment of truth, realizing that there is only one solution to humanity's inner unrest. Explaining mankind's inborn desire to seek God and to praise Him, Augustine wrote, "You have made us for Yourself, and our hearts are restless until they find their rest in You."[1]

There it is in a nutshell: The place of ultimate rest is found nowhere else but in relationship with God. We are made in the image and likeness of our heavenly Father, and we all share an abiding need to be in close communion with Him. Every good thing that comes into our lives—whether the love of family or the beauty of God's creation or the wonder of His work in our midst—none of these will come close to quieting our restless hearts.

God wants to refresh your soul—to replace anxiety with peace, to give you rest in place of weariness, to provide a place of belonging that will quiet your restlessness. In other words, God wants you to find contentment in His love and grace.

Why is it, then, that we insist on trying all the temporary, earthly "solutions" to our discontent? It seems our human nature is given to restlessness, even when that means turning our back on God. Hymn writer Robert Robinson eloquently described this human tendency:

O to grace how great a debtor
Daily I'm constrained to be!
Let Thy goodness like a fetter
Bind my wand'ring heart to Thee.
Prone to wander—Lord, I feel it—
Prone to leave the God I love;
Here's my heart, O take and seal it,
Seal it for Thy courts above.

This is the third verse of a great hymn, "Come, Thou Fount" (composed by John Wyeth). Sadly, the words were prophetic of the author's personal struggles. Toward the end of his life, Robinson lapsed into sin and false doctrine. One day while he was riding in a stagecoach, a woman began to hum a tune and asked Robinson if he knew the song. He replied tearfully, "Madam, I am the poor unhappy man who wrote that hymn many years ago, and I would give a thousand worlds, if I had them, to enjoy the feelings I had then."[2]

Our modern epidemic of discontent is an age-old problem with the search for a solution that takes us back to our original ancestors, Adam and Eve. Let's turn the page and start at the beginning.

THE DESIRE TO FLEE

Our lack of contentment keeps us moving—if not always geographically, at least internally. The longing for contentment produces an inner restlessness fed by the belief that we'll never really be satisfied where we are. We suspect the answer is just beyond the next bend in the road and someday we'll reach the hoped-for destination. At least, that's our expectation.

In the first book of the Bible, the first sign of human restlessness appeared when Adam and Eve sinned against God. The shame they felt after their disobedience brought an uneasiness, a lack of peace, and an unsettledness to their life. Those traits became more than simply feelings when God cast them out of the Garden of Eden. Now they were forced to set up housekeeping outside paradise. They remained near the garden, but they constantly sensed their loss of intimacy with God. Their sin put distance between them and their Creator.

As we read further in the Old Testament, we see that other people widened this distance between God and humanity. They chose not to live according to God's requirements, so in rebellion they built cities and even created civilizations in opposition to His rule. They were intent on seeking contentment in things other than God—with tragic consequences, as we will see.

One

THE ROOT OF DISCONTENTMENT

Learning the Story That Explains Our Restlessness

Adam suppressed a shudder as he listened to his wife's scream. *How much more could she take of this?* he wondered. *How much more could he take?*

Eve had suffered for hours, and her prolonged agony threatened to exhaust Adam's sympathy. One of his arms was bruised where Eve had gripped it in pain. His other arm was weary from waving a palm frond over his wife's sweat-soaked body. As the day wore on, Adam began to wonder if the child his wife carried would ever come forth from the womb.

When her latest cry subsided, Eve went limp and closed her eyes. But Adam knew her reprieve from the pangs of childbirth would be short-lived. After a long silence, Eve looked at her husband.

"It wasn't supposed to be this way, was it?" she asked.

Adam shook his head. "No," he replied, his voice hoarse from fatigue. "It wasn't supposed to be this way."

He pushed a lock of damp hair off Eve's forehead, then leaned back against a tree and closed his eyes. It grieved him that the sweet pleasure of intimate union with his wife now led to such travail. Adam had witnessed many animals giving birth, and the process had never seemed this torturous. His head—as well as his heart—ached for his wife over the pain she was suffering.

Eve squeezed desperately on his arm again, snapping Adam out of his reverie.

"I'm sorry," he whispered. He was sorry for her pain and sorry most of all that her pain was a consequence of their sin. If only they had obeyed the Lord.

Adam's thoughts wandered back to the day God banished them from the garden. The Lord had pronounced a curse on the pair, telling Adam that he would have to toil against weeds and brambles to produce enough food to feed his family.[1] The calluses on his hands offered proof of Adam's strenuous labor since that day.

To Eve the Lord had said, "I will greatly increase your pains in childbearing."[2] The couple was now witnessing the fulfillment of that prophecy. The joy and pride Adam had felt as he watched his wife's belly swell had turned to sorrow at her continued anguish. Eventually the ordeal came to an end when Eve's cries subsided with a final, wrenching push. There was no silence under the canopy, however. A noisy protest erupted from a small, red-faced being with clenched fists, and the lusty crying seemed to announce his fury at the trauma of being propelled into the world from the safety of his mother's womb.

In amazement Adam examined the tiny fingers and toes of his squalling son. The new father's exhaustion evaporated into a sense of wonder at this one-of-a-kind creature. Eve had once been a part of his own being, Adam reflected. Now this new infant, so small and so vulnerable, had come from Eve's body, and he would forever carry the imprint of both his parents.

As Eve gazed at her son, the haunted look of anguish faded from her face. She stroked his cheek, and the baby's wailing quieted to a whimper.

"With the help of the LORD," Eve said, "I have brought forth a man."[3]

For a few minutes the mother communicated wordlessly with the tiny child cradled in her arms. Then Eve turned to her husband and asked, "What name will you give him?"

Adam thought for a moment. He had named all the animals God had created; now he had the privilege of naming this unique individual.

"I will call him Cain," Adam finally said, giving the child a name that echoed Eve's declaration that she had "brought forth" a son.

Eve nodded her agreement. "We will teach you well, Cain," she said to the newborn. "We will teach you God's commandments so you will not make the same mistakes we did."

⌁

It might seem odd that we would study an ancient Bible story to find the explanation for our modern disease of discontent. But there is no other explanation for our restlessness. Our dissatisfaction in life began near the beginning of human history, when Adam and Eve first sinned against God. Their disobedience caused the human sin nature to be inherited by their own children and by every human born after them. Just as sin created distance between Adam and Eve and their Creator, our own sin moves us far from God and creates a lack of contentment. To understand the implications of our sin nature, we must look to the Garden of Eden and see life as our Creator designed it to be.

In the fictionalized account of Cain's birth that opens this chapter, Eve observed that "it wasn't supposed to be this way." It certainly wasn't. But everything changed the moment Adam and Eve chose to disobey God, and we are still living with the ramifications of their decision. Their sin erected a barrier between them and God, and it caused them to be cast out of the Garden of Eden. This break in relationship between God and humanity continues to this day, and it explains why contentment continues to elude us.

In my view, this makes the first few chapters of the Bible critically important to comprehend. You see, the Bible is a unified writing that presents a systematic and organized plan—an eternal plan. Not only does Scripture allow us to see what God has done in the past, but it also opens our eyes to what God is doing among us today and what He will be doing in the future. That's why it's essential to gain a clear picture of God's plan from beginning to end.

A Beginning That Mirrors the Ending

While God has no beginning and no end, He chooses to appear to us within the confines of time and space, to intervene in human history, and to make Himself understandable to humankind.

The Bible begins with God creating the universe. As He created matter out of nothing, He set aside a special place where He fellowshiped with Adam and then with Eve. It was an indescribably beautiful garden called Eden, and at the beginning Adam and Eve enjoyed unhindered communion with God. Scripture ends with the book of Revelation, which paints a picture of what is to come. Revelation describes the New Jerusalem, a magnificent and exquisite garden city that will come down from heaven.

History begins with a wedding between a man and a woman, and it ends with a symbolic wedding between the Bridegroom, the Lord Jesus Christ, and His bride, the church—the multitude of believers from every tribe, every nation, every tongue, and every age.

At the beginning, Genesis describes Adam and Eve being placed in the garden as God's deputies, and Revelation depicts Jesus' followers ruling and reigning with Him. The Bible begins with a man and a woman in a place of peace and tranquility and joy, and it ends with all believers in a place of far greater peace, infinite tranquility, and joy everlasting.

But just as the beginning mirrors the ending, there is much that happens in between. The witness of Scripture reveals not only the cause of our restlessness and loss of contentment, but it also leads us to the perfect solution that God provides. There is a place of peace, rest, and belonging—a place where our search comes to an end.

THREE LESSONS FROM THE GARDEN

When God created humanity, there was complete contentment. Adam and Eve lived in paradise, a place of perfect peace and protection.[4] As we try to imagine what such a place would be like, we gain three insights that clarify the difference between the lack of contentment and true peace.

1. Exquisite Beauty

To say that the garden of Eden was exquisitely beautiful would be a terrible understatement. We really have no words to describe the beauty and majesty of this garden.

Think of the most breathtaking panorama you've ever viewed. Perhaps you were standing on a mesa overlooking the immense majesty of the Grand Canyon...or standing below Niagara Falls, listening to the deafening roar of the massive rush of water...or watching the sun melt into the ocean as it set on the western horizon. You were awestruck at the glory of God's creation. Now multiply that sense of wonder a thousandfold—and you still cannot imagine the pristine beauty of God's garden.

As God created every part of the universe, He pronounced it "good." But He unleashed the full extent of His creative power when He designed a garden home for Adam and Eve. For them, He poured out beauty beyond our comprehension.

But this boundless beauty was soon spoiled. Just as pollution despoils the physical environment that God created for us, a different kind of pollution devastated the Garden of Eden. When sin entered the garden, it spoiled the beauty of holiness. Through man's disobedience, sin gained a foothold in God's garden and turned it from paradise into a spiritual garbage dump.

Sin turns innocence into shame and joy into drudgery. Sin transforms purity and perfection into cynicism and faithlessness. It does everything in its power to destroy the exquisite beauty that God creates. Sin explains our loss of peace.

2. Abundant Provision

The Garden of Eden was not beautiful only in the aesthetic sense. Its beauty was functional. It was amazingly productive. The trees were pleasing to the eye and also good for food. As part of God's plan of provision, He assigned Adam the job of maintaining the garden.

People often have the mistaken notion that paradise implies inactivity. They assume that before the Fall Adam and Eve had nothing to do. But they didn't just lounge around all day—they had work to do. "The LORD God took the man and put him in the Garden of Eden to work it and take care of it."[5] Adam, and later Eve, had important work to do, but they were working *inside* the garden, in the presence of God, and that made all the difference. Work inside the garden was a delight. God gave them satisfying work so they would find fulfillment in it. Later, after sin stole their purity and innocence, their work moved *outside* the garden. They learned what it was to toil and labor with difficulty just to produce their daily food.

Before the Fall an atmosphere of sweet harmony pervaded the garden. Adam and Eve were in harmony with each other and in harmony with their environment because they were in harmony with God. That's what made Eden a paradise, and it helps us comprehend their complete contentment.

3. Complete Protection

Just as the garden's beauty and provision teach us about contentment, its ability to protect its occupants also demonstrates an essential element of contentment. The enclosed nature of the garden tells us much about the quality of life there. The walls that surrounded the garden are symbolic of

God's protection. He sheltered Adam and Eve within the walls, guarding them from all danger. Although the garden was enclosed, it was open from above, where God's watchful eyes were constantly upon them.

Within the walls of the garden, Adam and Eve walked and talked with God. They fellowshiped with their Creator and enjoyed His protection. This same relational God longs to fellowship with you, too. Take time to talk with God, and He will talk with you. You can know God's heart by reading His Word. And when you fellowship with Him, you have His divine protection.

While Adam and Eve had always enjoyed complete protection in the garden, they fell for the serpent's deception and exposed themselves to danger. In the middle of the garden, God placed a special tree. It wasn't an apple tree, as the popular misconception goes. It was called the Tree of the Knowledge of Good and Evil, and God instructed Adam and Eve not to eat the fruit of this tree.

> The LORD God commanded the man, "You are free to eat from any tree in the garden; but you must not eat from the tree of the knowledge of good and evil, for when you eat of it you will surely die."[6]

Contrary to the serpent's assertions when he confronted Eve, eating the fruit of this tree would not bring her the knowledge of good and evil. Rather, the ability to distinguish between good and evil could only come from obeying God's command and *not* eating of this tree.

Temptation always brings a choice. It is an opportunity either to come under God's authority and have victory over the temptation or to go our own way and suffer defeat. Temptation reminds us that alone we are helpless victims, but with the Lord we are conquerors. God's victory over sin is our protection.

A SECOND GARDEN

God used a second garden to confirm His perfect plan to give us victory over the sin that was born in the Garden of Eden. That second garden was the Garden of Gethsemane.

In the first garden the first man rebelled against God by disobeying His command. But in the second garden, Jesus, the perfect God-man, obeyed the Father fully. Satan got the upper hand in the Garden of Eden. But in the Garden of Gethsemane, Jesus submitted to His Father's will, which guaranteed Satan's defeat.

When Adam and Eve ate the forbidden fruit, their disobedience infected all of humanity with the virus of sin. But Jesus' perfect obedience led from the Garden of Gethsemane to the Cross, making it possible for His followers to be forgiven of their sins. If you are not walking in the power of the One who defeated sin, then sin is defeating you. Living outside the authority of God will bring nothing but worry, fear, and anxiety.

Just as one tree of temptation held sway over Adam, it was on a tree that Jesus was crucified, taking back the sting of sin and death. On the tree of Calvary, Jesus gave us the hope of heaven.

〜

Because of their sin, Adam and Eve had to leave the sheltering safety of the garden and make a life for themselves in the outside world. While they continued to dwell near the Garden of Eden, their oldest son, Cain, became a wanderer and eventually built a city founded on man's rebellion. Taking a look at the city of man will give us added insight into our struggle with a lack of contentment.

Two

BUILDING A PLACE TO HIDE

The Rootless Attraction of the City

The woman stood at the tent's open flap, her arms folded across her ample midsection, and stared at the lone man sitting in front of a dying campfire. "Come inside," she called to him. "It's late, and the others have all left."

Cain turned and looked in the direction of the voice. The night was cloudy, and in the dim firelight he could barely make out the bulky figure of his wife. But the note of complaint in her voice left no question as to her identity or her intent.

A familiar anger rose in his chest, but he remained silent. After kicking dirt over the fire, he strode to the tent and shoved his wife aside as he entered. When she caught the tent flap to keep from falling, Cain grabbed her arm and yanked her inside.

"You ignorant fool," he shouted. "You almost pulled the tent down around our heads."

"You p-pushed me…," she began to protest, then stopped, realizing the danger of saying more. Silently she sat on the sleeping mat, keeping a protective hand over her stomach.

Cain paced the short distance from the door of the tent to the mat and back. "What business do you have trying to dictate my every move?"

His wife chose not to respond, and her silence fueled Cain's anger. He leaned down and raised her chin with his open hand. "Answer me!" he hissed.

She trembled at his touch and immediately began pleading for mercy. "Please don't hit me. Think of the baby."

Cain crossed his arms to restrain his violent impulse. He didn't want to harm the child, especially if it happened to be a son. A man needed sons.

The woman lay on the mat and covered her face with her hands. "I wish I had stayed behind," she cried. "I should never have come with you."

Cain snorted his disgust. "What is it you want from me?"

She took a deep breath, as if summoning courage, and said, "If kindness and compassion are too much to ask, then can I at least find companionship? I'm far from home, and I'm frightened and lonely."

"Lonely? You're surrounded by people all day long."

"Yes, there are people, but I'm still lonely…in here." She motioned to her heart. "The other women don't like me; they just try to get close to me because you're the leader and they hope to curry favor. And you're gone from sunup until sundown, building a wall around the camp…"

"I'm building a city—for us, for our children," he interrupted.

She continued as if he hadn't spoken. "When it's too dark to work any longer, you sit by the fire with the other men, telling stories until the moon is high in the sky. Most nights you wait until I'm asleep before you come to bed. I'm lonely for you…" Her voice trailed off, as if she were either too embarrassed or too overwhelmed to continue.[1]

Cain sighed and ran his fingers through his hair. Anger and frustration, not to mention hours of grueling work, had left him exhausted. "Get some sleep," he said more harshly than he intended.

When he finally heard his wife's deep, even breathing, Cain quietly left the tent. If the moon had been shining brightly, he would have walked along the stone wall that was his consuming passion. Soon his men would have the entire camp enclosed, then they would begin work on permanent dwellings. No more living in tents.

And no more wandering.

Cain could not help smiling at that thought. He savored the feeling of triumph. *I have broken God's curse,* he thought. *I am no longer a restless wanderer. I am the builder of a city.*

The city would offer protection and security. They would have no need of God. Cain would have many children, and those who had come with him would have more children, and soon the city would grow into a thriving community. He would be its leader, and he would be accountable to no one.

A breeze stirred, and Cain heard the whisper of leaves overhead. The sound gave him a sudden chill, and for the briefest of moments he thought he heard his brother's voice. "Your brother's blood cries out to me from the ground," God had said.[2]

With great effort, Cain forced thoughts of the past from his mind and returned to his plans for the future. In his city there would always be something to do and always someone to talk to, even in the dead of night. Cain would never have to be alone with his thoughts again, and that was reason enough to build a great city.

⌣

Adam and Eve finally owned up to their sin, and they regretted the break in their relationship with God. But not so their son Cain.

In spite of his parents' conscientious teaching, Cain's disobedience far surpassed that of Adam and Eve. The story of how Cain murdered his younger brother, Abel, is familiar even to people who have never picked up a Bible, as is the defiant question Cain asked God: "Am I my brother's keeper?"[3]

Human disobedience had very quickly produced the first homicide, the most violent of crimes. It's interesting to notice what led to the murder. Cain was angry that God accepted Abel's offering while rejecting his own. The loss of contentment can extend to an overwhelming distrust of God.

Cain brought an offering to the Lord from his harvest. Abel also brought an offering, the firstborn from his flock. The brothers' offerings were consistent with their occupations: Cain tilled the ground and Abel raised sheep. Outwardly, both brothers seemed to be performing a righteous act. But Cain wanted to approach God on his own terms.

The Bible doesn't specify how either brother knew whether his offering was accepted or rejected by God, but it's clear that they understood the outcome—it was the reason for Cain's anger and jealousy. "The LORD looked with favor on Abel and his offering, but on Cain and his offering he did not look with favor. So Cain was very angry, and his face was downcast."[4] God issued a stern warning, telling Cain that sin was lying in wait for him. But God also offered mercy, making it clear that if Cain did what was right, he would be accepted. Cain refused to heed God's warning. Instead, he enticed his younger brother into a field where he attacked him and beat him to death.

Unlike Adam and Eve, who first tried to make excuses for their sin in the Garden, Cain's reaction was outright denial. When God confronted him with the fact of his brother's murder, Cain responded with defiance, saying he knew nothing about it.

As punishment, Cain was doomed to leave the land of Eden to become "a restless wanderer on the earth."[5] Scripture is silent regarding just how long Cain lived a nomadic lifestyle, but it does say that when Cain's wife gave birth to their son Enoch, "Cain was then building a city, and he named it after his son."[6]

RESTLESS WANDERERS

Like Cain, many people today are running from God. Perhaps they are not even aware that they are wandering spiritually. And like Cain, many people take refuge in a city in an attempt to quiet their restlessness. Some of them are running away from people or perhaps their own past. Others are desperately looking for something to fill an inner void—even though they may not be able to express what it is they're searching for. All they know is that they have no peace.

But running from God will never alleviate the guilt of sin. Only one remedy exists for the pain and suffering caused by sin, and that is found in facing up to our shortcomings. The way to deal with sin and guilt is through confession and repentance.

Cain was given a chance for repentance, but he chose to reject God's mercy. Instead, he tried to run from God and build his own city—and each generation of his descendants living in that city reached a new level of wickedness. Following the example of Cain and taking refuge in the city of man will never bring peace to our restless hearts. The peace we yearn for can be found only in the garden of God's grace.

In chapter 1 we looked at three important characteristics of the Garden of Eden: It was a place of exquisite beauty, abundant provision, and complete protection. Now let's contrast the garden of God with the city built by man.

The City of Man

People often move to a large city to escape the boredom of a small town. It's true that the city offers greater opportunities for employment and education plus fine restaurants, shopping, and entertainment. But there are also problems associated with living in an urban area: pollution that fouls the air, higher crime rates, and fear for personal safety. And the high-paying job that seemed so attractive can be lost instantly in a massive layoff when the financial markets go sour.

Contrast that with the Garden of Eden. There was no pollution. Fear and anxiety didn't exist because God was their Protector. There was no possibility of economic collapse because God was their Provider. God intended for us to live in the unspoiled environment of the garden, but man chose to wander away from God and build a city.

Restlessness led Cain to build a city, and his restlessness resulted in rootlessness. This is the first characteristic of the city of man.

Rootlessness

After being evicted from the garden, Adam and Eve remained nearby, living in the land of Eden. They not only stayed in close physical proximity to the garden, they stayed close to the presence of God. Their lives remained rooted in God.

After Adam and Eve sinned, God provided a covering made of animal skin for their nakedness. They accepted the fact that God had shed the blood of an innocent animal to cover the shame of their sin.[7] This was the first instance of the shedding of blood to cover sin, and it would find its ultimate and final expression on the Cross of Christ.

Adam and Eve taught the principle of animal sacrifice to their children, but Cain wanted to approach God on his own terms. He wanted to give God what *he* thought God should get, not what God required. Therefore, when God rejected Cain's offering of grain, Cain was unrepentant and wound up rootless, wandering away from God.

Cain's modern-day equivalent is the occasional churchgoer who wants to be a Christian on his own terms, not on God's terms. He clings to the notion that his good deeds can save him, because he doesn't want to come to God through the blood of the Cross. Such people may go to church every Sunday, but they are spiritually rootless and doomed to restlessness.

Loneliness

In a large city you find masses of people, of course. Yet a significant proportion of them, perhaps the majority, feel a deep sense of loneliness. Uncomfortable with being alone, people tend to hide in numbers. They congregate in groups, harboring the illusion that they are connected to others. But most of them share little more than a passing acquaintance.

Most people concentrate on their own interests, hardly thinking of others. Even husbands and wives can feel like strangers living under the same roof because they don't know how to experience true intimacy. We are often too afraid to look in our own hearts, let alone share our thoughts and feelings with another person—even if that person has pledged to love and care for us. Being intimate means opening up to one another and being vulnerable, and that's a risk many people are not willing to take.

This is not the way God meant for us to live. He designed us to need each other. In the garden, Adam and Eve fellowshiped with God. They enjoyed each other's company, and they shared the enjoyment of intimate communion with God.

Contrast that to the city of man. When you look at the descendants of Cain described in Scripture, you have to conclude that Cain's city was full of lonely, hard, arrogant, self-seeking people. This is because choosing a self-directed life instead of obedience to God leads to loneliness and isolation. It steals our contentment. On the other hand, opening our heart to God and to others leads to connection, companionship, and peace.

Superficiality

Life in the city of man breeds superficiality, which feeds isolation and loneliness. For five generations the inhabitants of the first recorded city grew progressively more self-absorbed and wicked. Take, for example, Lamech, one of Cain's descendants.

Lamech married two women, Adah and Zillah, whose names symbolize the superficiality of those who dwell in the city of man.[8] The name Adah refers to pleasure or sensation, and Zillah means "luxuriant hair covering." Zillah bore Lamech a daughter named Naamah, and her name has the connotation of sensuality.

These names describe a culture committed to outward appearances and the pursuit of pleasure. While there is nothing wrong with beautiful people or beautiful things, a culture can become obsessed with the superficial. And when a society worships superficiality—when beauty becomes a god—there is no place for genuine spirituality.

We live in such a culture today. We're obsessed with athletes, movie stars, and supermodels. People carry this obsession to such an extreme that some have proposed creating designer babies by using carefully selected ova from fashion models—our culture's "beautiful people." A few years ago a report surfaced on the Internet that a Web site was offering to auction off the eggs of models to infertile couples. The report created a firestorm of controversy. It's not known whether the site, dubbed Ron's Angels, ever succeeded in making a sale. The curious must pay a monthly subscription fee just to access the descriptions of the models and find out the purchase price of their respective eggs. The entrepreneur who created the Web site has been associated with a number of pornographic sites and may simply have been using it as a means of directing subscribers to sexually explicit materials.[9] But the mere fact of its existence is a disturbing commentary on the extent to which our society is sold out to the superficial.

What moral sickness would give rise to the idea of producing children based on superior physical appearance? No wonder some public schools have had to reinstate curricula that teach values like honesty and integrity, honor and faithfulness, compassion and generosity—attributes that have become endangered species in our image-driven society.

Pride and Arrogance

The inhabitants of the city of man were ruled by pride and arrogance, refusing to be accountable to anyone—least of all God. In such an amoral climate, violence runs rampant and justice is perverted.

Do you think gangsta rap, which glorifies violence and demeans women, is something new? Far from it. The mind-set that birthed this musical genre can be traced back to Cain's descendants. The fourth chapter of Genesis records a song in which a vengeful Lamech boasts of inflicting violence on his enemies. We have no idea, of course, what this primitive song sounded like, but the meaning of the lyrics is obvious:

> Adah and Zillah, listen to me;
>> wives of Lamech, hear my words.
> I have killed a man for wounding me,
>> a young man for injuring me.
> If Cain is avenged seven times,
>> then Lamech seventy-seven times.[10]

In the Hebrew language, these words come across as defiance against God. Lamech might as well have been saying, "God does not run the world according to my preferences, so I'll take things into my own hands. My justice is swifter than God's, and my judgment is better. God put a mark on my forefather Cain's forehead to protect him, but I can take care of myself, thank you very much."

Lamech's boasting would not sound that unusual in our modern context, in a society that suffers from a massive lack of accountability. Our culture is trying to overthrow all vestiges of authority—especially God's authority. There is no better example of this than the U. S. Supreme Court overturning a law prohibiting the practice of sodomy. Thus something the

Bible specifically prohibits is now legal throughout the land. And I don't need to cite examples of how violent our world has become, both on a broad scale, with global terrorism and weapons of mass destruction, and closer to home, with serial murders, drive-by shootings, and sexual and domestic violence.

I don't know when God's judgment will come, but He will not tolerate the wickedness of the city of man indefinitely. God will eventually say, "Enough is enough." And as He executes judgment, He will preserve a godly remnant of those who stand against the evil of their day.

That's exactly what we see in Scripture:

> The LORD saw how great man's wickedness on the earth had become, and that every inclination of the thoughts of his heart was only evil all the time. The LORD was grieved that he had made man on the earth, and his heart was filled with pain. So the LORD said, "I will wipe mankind, whom I have created, from the face of the earth—men and animals, and creatures that move along the ground, and birds of the air—for I am grieved that I have made them."[11]

What an amazing proclamation of punishment—the annihilation of all living beings, both human and animal! Notice the progression of wickedness, blossoming from that first sin in the Garden of Eden and growing to the point of complete depravity in the city of man. Yet God is not without mercy. The very next verse of Genesis 6 says, "But Noah found favor in the eyes of the LORD." [12]

Noah was from the lineage of Seth, the son born to Adam and Eve after Cain murdered Abel. Actually, Noah was the tenth generation after Adam and was the first person listed in Scripture who was born after Adam died at the age of 930.

We're all familiar with the story of Noah building an ark and loading it with his family and two of every animal on earth. While God brought judgment on the wickedness of humanity, He also preserved a faithful remnant of His people and even made gracious provision for the animal kingdom.

After the majority of the earth's population was wiped out during the Great Flood, Noah's descendants began to repopulate the planet. Yet because man retained his sin nature, peace and contentment did not prevail for long. Within several generations, man was again reaching for God on his own terms. In the following chapter, we'll examine a dramatic example of how one man's quest for greatness in building a tower to the heavens ended in disaster.

Three

COMPETING WITH GOD

Why We'll Never Find Contentment on Our Own

The king rose early and summoned his chamberlain just as first daylight broke over the plains of Shinar.

"I will visit the construction site today," the king informed his chief palace official. "Send a messenger to alert the supervisor that I will arrive shortly and that I expect a full accounting for the delay."

Nimrod quickly dismissed the chamberlain, who left to dispatch a messenger. Two attendants stepped forward to assist the king with his robes.

A scowl deepened the lines on Nimrod's forehead. The tower project was taking much longer than it should, and he wanted to know why. If nothing else, a personal visit from the king would spur the foremen to push their crews harder.

I've built entire cities, Nimrod complained silently as he traveled through the city of Babylon, *but nothing has taken as long as this tower. And nothing has been as important to me.*

The tower would be his crowning achievement, a beacon to draw people to the center of his kingdom. The architects and astrologers had aligned the rising structure with the stars—ensuring its destiny, they told the king—and there would be a chamber at the top where the royal stargazers could observe the heavens and offer sacrifices to their gods. Nimrod cared nothing for their gods, but he didn't discourage the superstitions of his subjects. On the contrary, their beliefs knit them together, and the tower would guarantee that the people would remain in the plains of Shinar rather than scattering beyond the great rivers.

As he approached the tower, Nimrod's sour mood improved slightly. The ziggurat[1] was an engineering marvel, a series of graduated rectangles stacked on top of one another and soaring into the sky. The pyramid had reached a height of seven stories so far, but it would be twice that when completed.

For a moment Nimrod stood and admired the architectural wonder. Hundreds of men walked single file up a steep ramp that rose around the sides of the tower and spiraled to the top. Groups of workers struggled with heavy ropes, pulling wooden skids loaded with bricks up to the new level under construction. Nimrod could hear the rhythmic chanting of the work crews as they unloaded a pallet of bricks and set to work.

The project supervisor approached the king respectfully if not quite reverently, and the king greeted the bulky man by name. Nimrod had chosen him to manage the project because of his expertise, but the king also appreciated the man's intimidating demeanor.

"If the great king would indulge his humble servant," the supervisor said, "I have called for the chief architect and astrologer to join us. We have good news for your majesty."

The conversation with the architect, astrologer, and project supervisor began with a cordial but businesslike tone, then deteriorated into a heated discussion, with the king waving aside their long-winded explanations before demanding details of their plan to get the project back on schedule.

"You promised me good news," Nimrod complained to the supervisor, "yet I've heard nothing but excuses."

With a motion to silence the others, the supervisor outlined their plan. "We will increase the number of conscripts, and we have identified all the current workers who are skilled both in brickmaking and bricklaying. We can assure your majesty there will be no further delay."

Nimrod leaned forward, fixing the supervisor with a penetrating stare. "Can you assure me of that…even if your life depends on it?"

The threat was not lost on the supervisor, who paused and cleared his throat before answering. He nodded his head affirmatively, but his words were unintelligible.

Nimrod looked at him quizzically, and the man repeated his answer twice, then seemed startled by the king's response.

"Speak plainly," Nimrod shouted, rising to his feet. "I command you!"

The supervisor tried to answer again, but this time his words sounded like gibberish. The king turned to the architect. "What do you have to say?"

The man shook his head and shrugged, muttering words the king was unable to comprehend.

"What's happening?" Nimrod asked the astrologer, who simply looked stunned, as if he couldn't understand the question.

A shouting match ensued, with each man talking and gesturing, but with none of them understanding the others. The insanity continued until they heard a loud crash from the direction of the tower.

In spite of his size, the supervisor moved swiftly, running outside to investigate. Nimrod and the others followed, and the king saw that a skid of bricks had fallen off the tower and pinned two men on the ground below. One of the victims appeared dead; the other was alive, but his leg was crushed. He cried out in agony as workers began to remove the bricks that had buried him.

Nimrod heard one of the masons ask, "What happened?" and the king was relieved to understand both the question and the injured man's answer.

But the supervisor evidently didn't comprehend; he began talking to the workers, gesturing toward the pile of debris, a look of near panic on his face.

Nimrod then realized that many of the workers were also speaking gibberish. He could understand a few of them, but the others spoke languages the king had never heard. The crew managed to extract the injured man and tend to his wounds, but the massive confusion had delayed their progress.

As the day wore on, the situation worsened. It seemed the Ninevites could converse with other Assyrians but not the Babylonians, and neither group could understand the Akkadians.

At sunset Nimrod returned to the palace, disheartened and exhausted. The work that had been proceeding in an orderly, if not timely, manner had now devolved into utter chaos. The next day the king summoned an elderly astrologer. At least the wizened man spoke plainly as he suggested that perhaps an unusual alignment of the heavenly bodies had caused the phenomenon of strange languages. Over the next few nights the astrologer consulted the stars and offered sacrifices to Marduk. But in the end the old man had neither an explanation nor a cure for the sudden muddling of languages.

With bitterness, Nimrod realized that his magnificent tower would never reach into the heavens. And as he had feared, the people began to scatter from his self-proclaimed center of civilization in Babylon, dividing themselves into tribes according to their new languages.

↜

The story of God confusing the languages at the Tower of Babel is a familiar one. What is less familiar is the rebellion that motivated the tower's construction. Nimrod's attempt to build the famed tower in ancient Babylon is a symbol of human effort to find contentment apart from God.[2] This event dates to ancient times, but it might surprise you to know there is a Babylonian revival in our own time.

What is most amazing about the resurgence of ancient pagan spirituality is that it is taking place in historically Christian countries—in Europe, where the Reformation originated, and in the United States, where the Pilgrims risked their lives to build a nation founded upon the principles of God.

This pagan revival has fostered a host of popular fads, the most widespread being tarot cards, horoscopes, and psychic hotlines—not to mention Harry Potter mania. The price tag of this growing interest in pagan spirituality is astronomical in both its financial and spiritual impact, as many people have destroyed their lives by acting on advice from psychics and shamans. If they had only sought God's counsel, if they had searched the Word of God and learned why pagan practices are inherently dangerous, they could have been spared untold heartache.

The human tendency to seek out "spiritual" guidance—rather than God's will—is thousands of years old. As we examine the biblical account of Nimrod and the Tower of Babel, we see the danger of striving to quell our spiritual discontentment outside of God's plan for humanity. The only reliable spiritual guidance available to us is the unerring direction that comes from God.

REJECTING GOD AFTER THE FLOOD

In the last chapter we saw that God destroyed the earth in a great flood because of humanity's increasing wickedness. But one man, Noah, and his family were spared. The earth was repopulated through Noah's sons: Shem, Ham, and Japheth.

Genesis 9 recounts a disturbing story of Noah getting drunk after harvesting a vineyard. Ham exposed his father's sin and ridiculed him. As a result, Noah cursed Ham's son, Canaan, the ancestor of the wicked nation later known as the Canaanites. "Cursed be Canaan!" Noah said. "The lowest of slaves will he be to his brothers."[3] Shem, on the other hand, honored his father, earning a blessing for himself and his descendants, including Abraham. It is from the name Shem that we get our term *Semite*, which still is used to describe the descendants of Abraham.

As we look at the pagan civilization of Babylon, however, we shift our focus to one of Ham's descendants, a "mighty warrior" named Nimrod.[4] The description doesn't imply that Nimrod was a military man, rather that he was the founder of a "power state." History chronicles the rise of the mighty kingdoms that succeeded one another in becoming the dominant force in the world at a particular time.

Nimrod mocked God and scorned the curse on his forefathers. He was a proud man and a powerful king who couldn't comprehend serving anyone, let alone becoming a slave to the descendants of Shem. So Nimrod attempted to prove that he had no need of God. In fact, he devoted his life to building a civilization in opposition to God's principles.

Nimrod's tower was, in many ways, the next step in a progression of rebellion that we've been tracing throughout the early generations of humankind. Adam and Eve sinned but settled near the Garden of Eden, remaining close to God's presence. Cain murdered his brother and then ran from God, settling farther to the east in the land of Nod, where he built a city.[5] Nimrod took this progression of sin several steps further, establishing an entire civilization in opposition to God.

Nimrod could have repented and turned to the Lord. Then, instead of receiving the curse of his ancestors, he would have found God's favor. But he refused to come to God for freedom from the curse because it would have required subjecting his will to God's will. It would have required Nimrod to relinquish sovereignty of his heart and mind to the divine purpose. And that was the one thing he could not do.

This same arrogant mind-set continues to rule those who refuse God's authority. Every disease and sickness known to humanity, every heartache and every pain, is the result of original sin. Yet we reject Christ's

sacrifice that brings us salvation, and we strive to conquer sin's consequences in our own strength, on our own terms. We believe that given
enough money and time, enough research and technology, we can do anything. We place our trust in science and supercomputers and declare that
we don't need God. Technology has become our god.

Nimrod's actions reflect this same attitude. He made a god of his own
ambition and pride, but he found out the hard way that God's decrees
cannot be defied forever.

THE CIVILIZATION THAT OPPOSES GOD

Babylon is the name of the civilization Nimrod built, and the Tower of
Babel typifies it. At the beginning of this chapter, a fictionalized story
paints a picture of how God's supernatural intervention against the construction of this tower might have occurred. We may not know all the
details of the event, but we do know that God brought Nimrod's
grandiose construction project to a dramatic halt by confusing the languages of the people involved.[6]

The name Babel is of Akkadian origin, and it means "gateway to
god." The tower Nimrod built was a ziggurat, a type of religious structure
that became common in ancient Mesopotamia. Like the pyramids of
Egypt, a ziggurat was built in successive stages, but in a rectangular shape,
with an incline along each side leading to the top of the tower. The upper-
most level contained a chapel or room for storing sacred objects.
Astrologers may have also used the upper level as an observatory for study-
ing the heavens.

Aside from the Tower of Babel, the city of Babylon occupies a significant place in the Bible. From Genesis to the book of Revelation, Babylon is a symbol of not just independence from God but living at enmity
with God.

This dubious reputation was born when the inhabitants of Babylon said, "Come, let us build ourselves a city, with a tower that reaches to the heavens."[7] With that statement, the well-organized human opposition to God began, and that is why God's Word uses Babylon as a symbol of the abomination of earthly cities. The people of Babylon had a vision of a civilization with humans in charge instead of God. Let's look at three aspects of the ancient city of Babylon that help explain how humans attempt to make God obsolete in the world.

1. Formal Rejection of God

Nimrod envisioned a great empire with a religious system that would make God unnecessary. The Babylonians chose to reject the knowledge of the true God. And when people reject God, they embrace false gods, intentionally or not.

Perhaps you've heard sermons or read books about prophecies that refer to the "mystery of Babylon." In Revelation 17:5, Babylon is depicted as a woman with a mysterious title written on her forehead:

BABYLON THE GREAT

THE MOTHER OF PROSTITUTES

AND OF THE ABOMINATIONS OF THE EARTH

The mystery of Babylon refers simply to any institution, society, or nation that rejects biblical truth and chooses to follow falsehood. All worship of false gods and goddesses—in Egypt, India, Rome, and Greece—originated in Babylon.

2. Stealing God's Glory

When the Babylonians said, "Let us build...a tower that reaches to the heavens," they weren't referring to reaching heaven or touching the sky. If they had meant that, they would have at least started building in the mountains. But they built the tower in the valley of Shinar, which is almost at sea level.

"Reach the heavens" is a figure of speech. The implication is that the top of the building would be dedicated to the worship of the zodiac, the heavenly bodies. It was from Babylon that astrology, the belief that the stars and planets influence human affairs and events on earth, was passed on to the entire world.

The great pyramids of Egypt also were constructed in relationship to the stars. Even the Sphinx reflects the signs of the zodiac. The great statue has the head of a woman, symbolizing the zodiac sign Virgo (the virgin), and the body of a lion, symbolizing Leo. Virgo is the first sign of the zodiac, and Leo is the last. So the Sphinx, which means "joining," represents the meeting point of the zodiac.

The influence of astrology was pervasive. After four hundred years of slavery in Egypt, even the Hebrews had begun to believe and practice astrology. When the Lord brought them out of Egypt, He warned them against worshiping the stars.[8] Why? Because worshiping the stars is a disguised form of worshiping demons. In reality, those who look to the stars for the key to their destinies, and those who faithfully follow their horoscopes, are worshiping Satan and his demonic forces under the guise of the zodiac.

Notice Satan's modus operandi. Also called Lucifer, Satan was originally an angel in heaven. But he wanted to be equal to God, so he led a rebellion against the Supreme Being. As a result, Satan and one-third of the angelic host were cast out of God's presence. These are the "fallen angels," which became the demonic forces under Satan's rule.

After he was thrown out of heaven, Satan deceived Adam and Eve into doubting God and managed to get them thrown out of the Garden of Eden. Then Satan deceived Cain into worshiping in his own way rather than God's way, which led to Abel's murder and ultimately to the massive destruction of life by the Flood. Then Satan deceived Ham's descendants into worshiping the zodiac—actually the worship of demons—and caused their destruction.

Today we see Satan continuing this strategy of deception and destruction, desiring to steal God's glory for himself. And if the current Babylonian revival continues unabated, it will ultimately bring the wrath of God.

In its lofty grandeur, the Tower of Babel symbolized a perversion of the revelation of God's plan for redemption. Nimrod's ziggurat was an attempt to steal God's glory and give it to Satan. The Almighty could not allow the tower to stand because He will not share His glory.

3. Self-Worship in Place of Divine Worship

You may wonder what motivated the Babylonians to build such a tower. Genesis 11:4 provides the answer: "So that we may make a name for ourselves and not be scattered over the face of the whole earth." The tower was an egotistical endeavor to achieve world renown, a memorial to focus the people's attention on the centerpiece of their humanistic civilization. It was designed to glorify humans, not God.

Their instinct for self-preservation was understandable but misplaced. After all, self-preservation is God's gift to us, an innate drive to ensure our survival in the world. But Satan always sows deception and confusion, and he convinces people to take a gift and turn it into an idol. The Babylonians used their innate desire for self-preservation to build a monument to memorialize their own efforts and to glorify themselves. They turned God's gift of self-protection into an idol of self-worship.

MODERN IDOLS

It's easy to criticize the pride and shortsightedness of the ancient Babylonians. But consider that we continue worshiping idols today without even realizing it. The most dominant among the modern idols is the god of self. Our resources, our energy, our time—our complete focus—is on the self. Slick politicians make campaign speeches that cater to the powerful god of self. The advertising industry dedicates itself to feeding the god of self. We even have a magazine called *Self.* Pick up a dictionary and you'll find as many as three pages filled with words that begin with the prefix *self,* from self-absorbed to self-worth. How concisely that demonstrates our obsession with self!

Self-esteem has become the byword in education. For all age levels we have curricula designed to increase students' self-esteem. With all the emphasis on kids feeling good about themselves, however, their academic performance has failed to follow suit. The Third International Math and Science Study showed that American students performed dismally compared to students in other nations.[9] However, we can rest assured that even though our students are lagging behind academically, they are doing so with high levels of self-esteem.

Analyzing the implications of such studies, research scholar Dinesh D'Souza described self-esteem as "a very American concept, and Americans, perhaps more than anyone else in the world, tend to believe that feeling good about yourself is an essential prerequisite to performing to the best of your ability.... But does a stronger self-esteem make students learn better? This seems dubious."[10]

We pursue higher levels of self-esteem because we lack contentment. We sense there is more out there than what we're experiencing, and we seek ways to obtain it. In our discontented pursuit of a "better" self, we're not that different from the Babylonians. Our culture's worship of self is guaranteed to bring unwanted consequences. When the Babylonian council assembled to defy God and steal His glory, God assembled His own Council. The divine meeting is described in Genesis 11:6-7: "The LORD said, 'If as one people speaking the same language they have begun to do this, then nothing they plan to do will be impossible for them. Come, let us go down and confuse their language so they will not understand each other.'"

The decree issued from the Council of the Holy Trinity—Father, Son, and Holy Spirit—resulted in a massive communication problem that prevented the Tower of Babel from being completed. God's judgment always prevails, and those who continue to worship the god of self will always be frustrated and sometimes even destroyed.

With modern technology man builds great buildings, and these towering edifices engender great pride. When you stand on the ground and look up at the Sears Tower, it literally makes you dizzy. But when you fly above that same skyscraper, it looks insignificant. From God's perspective, all of humanity's intellectual and scientific achievements amount to nothing more than a pimple on the face of the planet.

Focusing on ourselves and our abilities—whether it's self-improvement or self-esteem or self-actualization—will produce the opposite of the contentment we long for. There is only one solution to our search for peace, for rest, and for lasting satisfaction. In the following chapters we will explore how humanity finds its contentment in God.

Part 2

LONGING TO FIND

After sin entered the human story, it took root and produced more extreme manifestations of rebellion against God. Inner restlessness gave way to pride, and people journeyed further and further from God's presence. Humanity hid from God, ran from Him, defied Him openly, and built civilizations in an attempt to replace Him with false gods.

But while many sought earthly contentment apart from God, there were others whose unsettled lives ultimately drove them into the Lord's presence. In the following two chapters we will examine the lives of David, Abraham, Ruth, and Joseph, whose faith caused them to discover earthly peace. Their wandering led them in the opposite direction of their ancestors. They ran *to* God instead of running *away* from Him. We will see that anyone, if he is willing, can turn restlessness into a passionate pursuit of God. That's when the search for contentment brings us back to God's heart.

FROM DESPERATION TO HOPE

How Our Deepest Needs Lead Us to God

How could my own son be plotting against me? the king wondered. He was fleeing the capital city with his entire household and the portion of his army that remained loyal to him. King David had faced many powerful foes before he assumed the throne and during his long reign. But this time it was his own flesh and blood who had launched a revolt.

Absalom, his oldest living son, had conspired to have himself crowned king in Hebron. David did not yet know how large an army Absalom had amassed, but the conspiracy was so widespread that even the king's trusted advisor, Ahithophel—Bathsheba's grandfather—had joined the rebellion. David decided to leave Jerusalem to avoid a bloodbath in the city when Absalom tried to seize the throne.

The king grieved silently as he rode his horse away from the city, picturing his son racing toward Jerusalem at the head of the rebel army. In the last few years, Absalom had acquired a chariot and horses plus fifty bodyguards. As he elevated his reputation in the kingdom, Absalom had taken pains to ingratiate himself with the people. David should have realized what his son was up to, but he had always had a weak spot toward Absalom.

David tried not to lose control of his emotions as he fled his home. He directed his men east, toward the desert. Villagers wept aloud as they watched the long procession pass by. Zadok and Abiathar, both priests, traveled with the caravan, and the Levites as well, carrying the ark of the covenant. No wonder the people wept as the army of Israel paraded in front of them, accompanied by the ark, the symbol of God's presence and power.

When he crossed the Kidron Valley, David allowed the army to go ahead of him. He remained with the priests while they offered sacrifices until all of David's entourage had left the city. Afterward, as the Levites prepared to take up the ark, David stopped them.

He called Zadok to his side. "Take the ark of God back into the city," he told the priest.

"But my lord—"

"No," David interrupted. "The ark belongs in Jerusalem. If I find favor in the Lord's eyes, He will bring me back and let me see His dwelling place again. But if He is not pleased with me, then I am ready. Let Him do with me whatever He will."[1]

Zadok relayed the king's command to the Levites, and they picked up the long poles that transported the ark. But the priest returned to David's side, prepared to go into exile with him.

"Go back into the city, and take Abiathar and your sons with you." Before Zadok could object, David said, "You are a prophet. Inquire of God for me. I will wait at the fords in the desert until word comes from you."[2]

With his heart heavy, David mounted his horse and turned east. He longed for a quiet place where he could pour out his grief to the Lord and seek guidance. What word would Zadok send to him? Would the Lord restore David's kingdom, or would his own son succeed in killing him?

David wept openly, as did many of his men, when the ark departed. He prayed that the Lord would turn Ahithophel's counsel to Absalom into foolishness.

They had not traveled far when Hushai the Arkite came to meet him. David's personal advisor had torn his robe and put dust on his head as a sign of mourning. "I have come to join you," Hushai said, "so that I may be of service to the king."

"If you come with me," David said, "you will only be a burden. But there is something you can do for me."

"I will do anything you ask, my king."

"Go back into the city and make yourself of great service. Do what you can to frustrate Ahithophel's advice. Pretend that you have changed your allegiance from me to my son. Whatever you hear in the palace, tell the sons of Zadok and Abiathar, the priests. They will bring word to me of what you learn."[3]

Hushai set off on his new mission, and David resumed his journey, wondering if God had begun to answer his prayer by making Hushai available. But David's tiny glimmer of hope dimmed as they neared Bahurim and a man named Shimei, from the clan of Saul, began to shout curses and pelt David's entourage with stones.

"Get out, you scoundrel," Shimei cried. "The Lord has repaid you for what you have done to the household of Saul. He has handed the kingdom over to your son Absalom because you are a man of blood!"[4]

David's heart was pierced by Shimei's words. He restrained his men when they wanted to cut the man's head off. *Perhaps the Lord had told Shimei to curse me,* David thought.

The caravan bypassed Jericho and traveled near Gilgal, finally stopping at the shallow tributaries of the Jordan River, where David had said he would wait for word from Zadok. Exhausted, the king withdrew for privacy.

Finally alone, David gave vent to his grief. Shimei's words rang in his ears, and they called to mind the words of the prophet Nathan. Years earlier, when Nathan had confronted David about his adulterous relationship with Bathsheba and his subsequent battle strategy that guaranteed her husband's death, the prophet had said to the king, "The sword will never depart from your house."[5]

God had forgiven David, but the king was still living with the consequences of his sin and his failure to discipline his sons. *I should have seen this coming,* David realized, *but I have been a blind fool where my sons are concerned.*

It was far too late to make up for his mistakes, yet David couldn't stop his mind from going over the past. He should have severely punished his son Amnon for the rape of Tamar, Absalom's sister. If he had, perhaps Absalom would not have killed Amnon, and then Absalom would not have gone into exile. *And I should never have listened to Joab and brought Absalom home,* David told himself. *This is my reward for being so foolish. My own son wants to kill me.*

As dusk crept over the desert, David wept until his eyes were swollen. Only the Lord could help him now.

"Where are you, O God my Rock?" he cried out. "Why have you forgotten me?"[6]

While David wallowed in his sorrow, a deer approached the stream. The panting animal barely looked around before wading into the water and drinking greedily. In his days as a shepherd, David had seen that kind of desperate thirst before; the deer was in too much pain to stop and guard against any hunters.

David's tears began to dry as he watched the deer. The animal continued to drink as if its thirst would never be quenched. *I am that deer,* David thought, and the words of a song began to form in his head: *As the deer pants for streams of water, so my soul pants for you, O God. My soul thirsts for God, for the living God.*[7]

⤳

As we study David's life, we find ample reason for his periodic bouts of depression. Yet in all of his suffering, and in all of his candid questions and passionate expressions of vulnerability, we don't sense that David ever lost faith in God's power to make things right. If he was to die at his son's hand, at least David would die trusting in God's care and provision.

Depression is a significant problem in our culture, with an estimated 10 percent of the United States population being affected by depressive illness at any given time.[8] Christians often are ashamed to admit to dark periods of melancholy, when hope for improvement seems unrealistic and when a person wonders if life will ever again return to normal. The life of David, a man of great faith, should teach us that every life, at some point, enters a dark valley.

But David is far from the only example of this. Men and women we would consider "supersaints" have struggled mightily with depression and despair. In fact, almost anybody who responds to the call of God will one day face doubts and questions, difficulties and trials, that will lead him or her through the door of depression—perhaps to the point of despairing of life itself.

On Mount Carmel the great prophet Elijah defeated hundreds of false prophets who worshiped the Canaanite god Baal, but when Queen Jezebel threatened to kill Elijah, he ran into the desert and hid. In despair he prayed for God to let him die. " 'I have had enough, LORD,' he said. 'Take my life; I am no better than my ancestors.' "[9]

Jeremiah became known as the Weeping Prophet because he anguished over the sins of God's people and the judgment he foresaw coming as a result of their disobedience. The people didn't want to hear Jeremiah's message of impending doom. They heaped abuse on the prophet, and the king had him beaten and imprisoned. Still, Jeremiah was faithful to deliver God's word to the people. More than once he withdrew in defeat and asked God why he had even been born.

Cursed be the day I was born!
May the day my mother bore me not be blessed!

Cursed be the man who brought my father the news,
    who made him very glad, saying,
      "A child is born to you—a son!"
May that man be like the towns
    the LORD overthrew without pity.
May he hear wailing in the morning,
    a battle cry at noon.
For he did not kill me in the womb,
    with my mother as my grave,
    her womb enlarged forever.
Why did I ever come out of the womb
    to see trouble and sorrow
    and to end my days in shame?[10]

Like Jeremiah and other dedicated servants of God, David was going through a similar bout of depression. I thank God for David's depression and his response of faith in God. His hunger for God, even in the pit of despair, is a vivid demonstration of the biblical answer to the problem of depression. If we didn't have these godly examples from the Bible, we would more easily fall prey to drugs, alcohol, or the secular and pseudo-religious remedies that the world offers.

QUENCH YOUR SPIRITUAL THIRST

Psalm 42 is a beautifully poetic description of spiritual hunger that shows that the answer is a driving thirst for God. "As the deer pants for streams of water, so my soul pants for you, O God." [11]

Many commentators point out that the deer was panting because it had been chased by dogs. And this, of course, could be true. But let me offer a Middle Eastern perspective on this verse. It's very common for the deer in this part of the world to eat snakes. When they eat a poisonous snake, the venom diffuses through their organs and produces an intense, burning heat that drives them to find water. It's a desperate urge that compels them to seek out the nearest stream, where water, and lots of it, will alleviate the fever.

So it is with us in the moment of our deepest discouragement: Relief comes only when we thirst for God.

The psalmist does not offer us platitudes in Psalm 42. He cuts through the pat answers and religious gibberish and tells us that the only spring of water that will satisfy our desperate need is the Living Water. I can so easily picture David observing an exhausted deer—spent, feverish, and desperate for water. We must get to the same place David was as he considered his murderous son and his desperate state at that moment. For David, only the fountain of God could satisfy his spiritual thirst and alleviate his "emotional fever."

Notice that as David grieved over Absalom's violent scheming, he didn't call for a priest or a counselor. He didn't read texts on self-actualization. He thirsted for God. David knew that nothing less than God Himself could satisfy his troubled spirit.

That's where we all need to be: thirsting for God. Longing not for the trappings of religion but for God Himself. When you go to church, do you go to hear a compelling sermon or beautiful, inspiring music? Do you go because of the programs and activities or to see your friends?

Or do you go to meet God?

Millions of Christians have lost all interest in God while they seek relief in advice from horoscopes or self-help books. Sadly, they miss the first, most important step toward healing: the Living Water. Only a burning thirst for God will bring satisfaction.[12]

SEPARATION ANXIETY

Notice the words that describe David's desperate longing to be in God's presence. "My soul thirsts for God, for the living God. When can I go to meet with God?" [13]

As David fled Jerusalem, he was leaving behind the sanctuary of God in Jerusalem. He had sent the ark of God back to the city, and he felt the loss of this holy symbol of God's presence and power. David longed to be in the traditional place of worship but found himself in temporary exile to the east of Jerusalem, toward the desert area of Israel.

This separation from God increased David's mental and emotional agony. All he could do was weep tears of pain, tears of exhaustion, tears of grief, tears of despair.

Some people, especially men, consider tears a sign of weakness. But there is a blessed release in tears. Holding them back only increases our physical suffering as well as our emotional pain. If we refuse tears, we are refusing a God-ordained channel of restoration. Jesus said: "Blessed are those who mourn, for they will be comforted." [14] That's the promise of God!

There is a sorrow that leads to hope and peace and contentment. There is a balm in suffering when we are connected to Jesus. His name is a healing ointment that soothes our spirits. There are different seasons in our lives—times of weeping and mourning and times of laughter and dancing. If you are going through a season of tears, remember that "weeping may remain for a night, but rejoicing comes in the morning." [15]

As David poured out his soul to the Lord, he reclaimed his joy.

CHEER UP BY LOOKING BACK

In Psalm 42:4 we see David gaining encouragement by looking back. "These things I remember as I pour out my soul: how I used to go with the multitude, leading the procession to the house of God, with shouts of joy and thanksgiving among the festive throng."

David was a man of praise and was not reluctant to abandon himself in praise to the Lord, even in front of his subjects. And we can picture David looking back to his days of leading worship in Jerusalem as he waited for word on Absalom's murderous intentions. Likewise, it helps us overcome difficulty when we focus on the things God has done in our lives in the past. For instance, one of the best things you can do when you have a family argument is to get out the photo album. Look at the pictures that bring back pleasant memories. It's amazing how the simple act of looking back can change the atmosphere, how tensions can evaporate and allow healing to flow as we recall blessed times together.

God reminded His people again and again of His redeeming act of delivering them from slavery in Egypt. Moses wrote the first recorded worship song, a hymn of victory, after God parted the Red Sea and destroyed the pharaoh and his army. Many of the psalms focus on God as deliverer and recall instances when He saved His people from calamity. In Psalms 105, 106, and 107 we read lengthy recitations celebrating the Israelites' deliverance from Egypt. Reciting these psalms reminded the people of what God had done for them in the past—and therefore what He would do for them again.

The stories of deliverance were familiar to David, of course, and he looked forward to seeing God do a similar work of deliverance in his own life. As the king remembered God's goodness in the past, he let the Holy Spirit challenge his lagging soul.

> Why are you downcast, O my soul?
> > Why so disturbed within me?
> Put your hope in God,
> > for I will yet praise him,

my Savior and my God.
My soul is downcast within me;
therefore I will remember you
from the land of the Jordan,
the heights of Hermon—from Mount Mizar.[16]

Notice that David did not get stuck in the past. He revisited God's faithfulness to him and used those memories as a bridge to the future. He cheered himself up by looking back, but then he moved forward. Moving forward is the necessary next step after we review God's faithfulness in our lives.

I can imagine David's thought processes during this time. *All of my experience shows that God has not withdrawn from me nor abandoned me. So what makes me think He would abandon me now? I will put my hope in God, and I will praise Him once again.*

This was a positive self-admonition. David was feeling as low as the Jordan Valley. But he also remembered the heights of Mount Hermon, and he knew God could bring him from the valley to the mountaintop. David's prescription for depression didn't seek a remedy in earthly diversions. His remedy was to turn to God, to thirst after God, to put his hope in God.

For David, the time for grieving was over. He had been deeply distraught, but now he recalled the goodness and the mercy and the power of God. David might have recalled a certain occasion when God turned calamity into celebration. Before he became king, David once went out with his men to work in the field. They left their wives and children in the city of Ziklag. While they were gone, the Amalekite troops ransacked the city, set it on fire, and took all the women and children captive.

When David's men returned to the charred remains of Ziklag and found their wives and children missing, they were furious and wanted to stone David. That's not entirely surprising. When people are frustrated in their own lives, they often blame the man up front.

David was understandably distressed that his friends wanted to kill him. He needed help, and Scripture tells us where he turned: "David encouraged himself in the LORD his God."[17] David began to ask God's direction. Then he followed God's leading and pursued the raiders who had looted Ziklag. Two days later David and six hundred of his men defeated the Amalekites and recovered all the plunder that had been stolen, along with all the women and children.[18]

With his own son now seeking to kill him, recalling God's provision at Ziklag would have been enough to put David in a better frame of mind. He had experienced God's deliverance on numerous occasions, and calling those times to mind helped him stop grieving and move forward into victory.

Has a dark cloud moved in over your life? Is a dense fog settling over the valley of your existence? Get ready! God is about to part the clouds and shower you with blessings. If you have learned to find your contentment in obedience to God, and if you trust that God is able to shine His light into the midst of your dark clouds, then He will bring peace and order to your confusion. God will provide for you, bringing you "water out of the rock" to sustain you in difficult times.

CLIMB UP FROM THE DEPTHS

"Deep calls to deep in the roar of your waterfalls; all your waves and breakers have swept over me."[19]

I can picture David standing at the waterfalls of Mount Hermon, watching the raging water sweep over the precipice. The crashing roar was a vivid picture of the waves of grief that had befallen the king. His grief was threatening to drown him.

We've all experienced waves of despair. But did you know that even in the midst of your ocean of sorrow, God can give you a song? In spite of the waterfall engulfing him, David found a song to sing. "By day the

LORD directs his love, at night his song is with me—a prayer to the God of my life."[20] It is natural to sing when the day is bright and clear. When your health is good and things are going well, it's easy to sing. But nighttime is a different story. When the shadows deepen, every sound seems to be magnified, every creak of the floorboards is scary.

Yet the psalmist promised that in the dark hours of your life, God will give you a song. The book of Job, as well, describes God as One "who gives songs in the night."[21] The song that takes the fear out of the night is the song of God's grace. The grace of God is more than forgiveness, more than unmerited favor. Grace is the love of God poured out, heaped up, pressed down, shaken together, and running over. Grace is God's love reaching out, embracing, redeeming, and building up the soul.

Over the roar of the waters, God's grace called out to David and reminded him of the source of his strength. David referred to God as his Rock, something he had forgotten during the depths of his depression. "I say to God my Rock, 'Why have you forgotten me? Why must I go about mourning, oppressed by the enemy?' "[22] Here is my own paraphrase of what David was saying: "Although I don't feel this way right now, it doesn't change the fact that You are the firm ground on which my whole life rests. I may have felt as if You had forgotten me, but deep down I know that You will *never* forget me!" David realized that subjective feeling—his sorrow and grief—was not the same as objective reality. What the Lord had done for David before, He could and would do again.

How easily we forget that our enemy is hard at work to convince us that God has forgotten us. Satan does not usually attack his own. He prefers to wait until a soul is clothed with Christ before he makes his move. The devil can pass nicely as a church member. After all, he believes in God, he believes the Bible, and he knows Christ very well.

Has the devil ever slipped into the church pew beside you? Have you heard a voice whispering questions in your ear? "How much of the Bible do you really believe? Honestly, do you really think a loving God would consign people to hell?

"And look at all those hypocrites! If you had any backbone, you'd walk out of this place and never come back. You're a hypocrite if you don't! Do you really believe that hymn you're singing? 'God loves you and guides you.' Oh, really? Then why is your life such a mess? The fact is, God has forgotten all about you!"

Satan has a million accusing questions, but there is a way to meet his attacks. Isaiah 59:19 says, "When the enemy shall come in like a flood, the Spirit of the LORD shall lift up a standard against him" (KJV). Acting alone, we are no match for the devil. But Jesus is! And in the name of Jesus we can say, "Satan, you are a liar. I do love God and His people. I reject your accusations. God is my Rock and my Fortress and my Deliverer. I will sing for joy to the Lord and shout aloud to the Rock of my salvation."

SURVIVING SHAME

In Psalm 42:10 we get a glimpse of what made David's pain even worse—the taunting of others. "My bones suffer mortal agony as my foes taunt me, saying to me all day long, 'Where is your God?'" This is the second time David referred to the taunts of his enemies, echoing the words of verse 3.

Perhaps there is no emotion that ranks lower than shame, especially the shame of discovering what people are really saying behind our back. We can take pain and loss, we can take illness and tragedy, but shame and disgrace are much more difficult. Of all Jesus' suffering, the greatest pain He endured, next to separation from the Father, was the jeering of the crowd: "He saved others...but he can't save himself! He's the King of Israel! Let him come down now from the cross, and we will believe in him. He trusts in God. Let God rescue Him now."[23] The chief priests and elders weren't the only ones who taunted Christ. As our Lord hung on a cross between two criminals, even the robbers being crucified on both sides "heaped insults on him."[24]

Jeers and taunts can land with bone-crushing weight. That is why the concluding verse of Psalm 42 repeats verse 5: "Why are you downcast, O my soul? Why so disturbed within me? Put your hope in God, for I will yet praise him, my Savior and my God."[25]

Why am I down? David asked himself. *Because I am looking down.* But he knew the cure: "I will hope in God." Hoping in the grace of God was the only way to relieve his desperate thirst. He needed to plunge into the streams of Living Water and drink until his soul was satisfied. This was the rest and contentment he longed for and desperately needed.

Maybe you're thinking that your situation is somehow more severe—and perhaps it is. But God's principles don't change. The God who was David's Rock is still God today. And He is your Rock, just as He was the solid ground under David's feet when everything else was coming apart.

Consider another case of serious depression involving a man known to us all. A young Midwestern lawmaker suffered such deep depression that his friends thought it wise to keep all knives and razors away from him. The man had been prone to bouts of melancholy all his life, but this period of depression seemed especially dark. He had just broken off an engagement, and in the ensuing weeks he became too ill to attend sessions of the state legislature.

During this time he wrote a letter to his former law partner, saying, "I am now the most miserable man living. If what I feel were equally distributed to the whole human family, there would not be one cheerful face on the earth. Whether I shall ever be better, I can not tell; I awfully forebode I shall not. To remain as I am is impossible; I must die or be better, it appears to me."

But the lawyer did recover. Just a year later he wrote a letter of encouragement to a close friend, telling him: "Remember in the depth and even the agony of despondency, that very shortly you are to feel well again."[26] Over the next twenty years the man went through other periods of depression, but he learned to weather them all—even while he served as president of the United States during a time of grave national crisis.

Today Abraham Lincoln is remembered for his outstanding leadership and for his notably sad countenance, evident in the photographs of this beloved president. But his friends also knew Lincoln as a warm and humorous man, one who reached out to others who were suffering.

"Lincoln's depressions, whether they lasted for hours, days, weeks, or months always came to an end. Knowing this, he was able to encourage others. It would seem his own experience led him to believe that depression was not a permanent condition."[27]

FINDING TRUE HOPE

How can you, like David, move out from under the weight of difficult times by putting your hope in the Lord? Remember that when Scripture talks about hope, it's not a matter of simply hoping for a good outcome. You may hope for something without having any assurance of getting it. But the hope that a Christian has is a guarantee that the future is secure. Our hope is not in ourselves, nor in others, nor in circumstances. Rather, our hope is in the living Christ, and that hope cannot fail.

Paul wrote to the Christians in Rome: "We rejoice in the hope of the glory of God. Not only so, but we also rejoice in our sufferings, because we know that suffering produces perseverance; perseverance, character; and character, hope. And hope does not disappoint us, because God has poured out his love into our hearts by the Holy Spirit, whom he has given us."[28]

Notice the progression from suffering to perseverance to hope. When we find our joy in the Lord and in His Word and His will, then we will experience hope even in the midst of a seemingly hopeless situation. David may have fed on his tears and panted for the streams of water. His bones may have been crushed and his soul disturbed to the point of thinking that God had rejected him. But no more. *Enough blathering about Absalom's rebellion,* David told himself. He knew that giving in to the groaning and grief would get him nowhere. It was time to stop grieving and start trusting.

There comes a time when we simply have to stop making things hard for ourselves. God does not cast us down or cast us off. Why should we do that to ourselves? God did not intend for Christians to live a woeful, disappointed, lonely life. Believers have a living hope, yet we can only comprehend this hope when we learn to live a Spirit-filled life.

That doesn't mean we have to disguise our fears and anxiety with pious platitudes. We can weep and grieve openly and honestly, and with real hope we can look back to past triumphs and then move forward to new adventures and new victories in Christ.

When we live the Spirit-filled life, we can know contentment and peace. We learn to praise the Lord no matter what is going on around us. A Spirit-filled life will replace self-esteem with gratitude to God.

We must turn our back on the god of self. As long as Christians concentrate on maintaining a good self-image, the Spirit of God will leave them alone. As long as Christians are filled with other spirits—such as greed, fear, envy, pride, hostility, or selfish ambition—they cannot be filled with God's Spirit. God will allow us to run our lives if we insist on taking control, but He reserves His Spirit for those who, like David, come panting and thirsting for the Living Water.

When we start hungering and thirsting for God, our restless journey turns and begins taking us home to God's heart. When we tire of our life as it is, when our loss of contentment exhausts us, when we finally stop looking for answers in the material world, then we're ready to experience the peace of God and the power of His Spirit. That's when discontent does the work of bringing us back to the heart of God.

Five

THE PURSUIT OF PEACE

At Times, God Calls Us to Enter Foreign Territory

"You wanted to see me, Mother?"

At the sound of her son's voice, Bathsheba turned away from the parapet wall where she had been looking out over the City of David. Her heart overflowed with pride when she saw her son, the king, looking so regal. And a bit impatient, she thought, though he was trying hard not to show it.

"Thank you for coming," she said. "I know you have many responsibilities today."

Solomon clasped his mother's hands in his and kissed her on the cheek. "Yes, I do. But a wise king once told me to always obey my mother."

She smiled and gestured toward the long settee, which took up most of one wall of her small but luxurious bedchamber. "Please sit down," she said. Solomon hesitated, as if not wanting to settle in for a long conversation, so his mother added, "I have a gift for you. Something your father wanted you to have."

As she moved toward a nearby table, she continued. "I should have given you this a long time ago, but I was so consumed with grief when David died that I forgot about it. Much later I discovered it stored with some of my belongings. I started to give it to you then, yet I held on to it for some reason. It seemed I had so few of his personal things."

Solomon reached over and squeezed his mother's hand. "What is this mysterious gift?"

"It's something that was very precious to David, something he entrusted to me. I was afraid you might find it foolish and not cherish it the way he had."

Bathsheba released her son's hand and turned to pick up a well-worn leather bag lying on the table. She held it gently, almost reverently.

"A shepherd's pouch," Solomon said slowly. "Why did he want me to have his shepherd's pouch?"

"He wanted you to have what is inside it. 'When Solomon becomes king,' he told me, 'I want him to have this, so he will always remember.'"

Bathsheba fell quiet, then loosened the drawstring of the large bag and drew out its contents. A single stone, smooth and round, completely filled the palm of her small hand. She offered it to Solomon.

Realization began to dawn as he examined it. "Is this the stone…?"

"No, it's not the one that killed Goliath. It was one of the four stones your father didn't have to use." She saw that her son was genuinely touched by the gift.

"He tried to teach me to use a sling," Solomon said, "but I could never match his skill. I still remember the instructions he gave for picking the right stone, though. Not too small, or it would not inflict enough damage. But not too large, or it would be too heavy to throw with sufficient force."

Bathsheba continued her explanation of the stone's significance to David. "During the clamor that ensued after he killed the Philistine, David discarded the remaining stones from his pouch. On an impulse, though, he picked up one of the stones, deciding to save it as a memorial. 'My strength came solely from being faithful to the Lord,' he told me, 'and the few times I forgot that and followed my own path, I nearly lost everything.'"

Her voice softened as she said, "He meant me, you know. I nearly cost him everything." She did not dwell on the thought, grateful that the memory of their sin no longer caused the same anguish it once had.

"He told me the story of Goliath many times," Solomon said. "I still remember what he said to the giant who had terrorized Israel: 'This very day the Lord will deliver you into my hand, and I will strike you down. Then the whole world will know that there is a God in Israel.'"[1]

Solomon sounded so much like his father that it brought tears to Bathsheba's eyes. "I shouldn't have kept this from you, but it's fitting that you should have this memento. You have fulfilled your father's dream, and you've built a house for the Lord. It was the greatest desire of his heart to honor God in that manner.

"Let this stone remind you of your father," she said, "and most of all let it remind you that your strength comes from the Lord. Nothing you do on your own could ever equal the victories God will win for you if you stay faithful to Him."

As the king left his mother's chambers, Bathsheba prayed that he would not let his desires carry him away from the Lord but that, like his father, he would be a man after God's heart.

That afternoon, when the priests carried the ark of the covenant into the inner sanctuary, Bathsheba stood in an honored position in the outer court with the throngs of worshipers. After the priests withdrew from the Most Holy Place, the glory of the Lord descended as a cloud and filled the temple. The presence of God was so powerful that the priests could not perform their duties.

Finally, the king stood and blessed the assembly. "Praise be to the LORD, the God of Israel, who with his own hand has fulfilled what he promised with his own mouth to my father David. For he said, 'Since the day I brought my people Israel out of Egypt, I have not chosen a city in any tribe of Israel to have a temple built for my Name to be there, but I have chosen David to rule my people Israel.'

"My father David had it in his heart to build a temple for the Name of the LORD, the God of Israel. But the LORD said to my father David, '...Your son, who is your own flesh and blood—he is the one who will build the temple for my Name.' The LORD has kept the promise he made."[2]

⤸

Solomon's speech at the dedication of the temple stands for all time as a tribute to God's faithfulness. Not only had God delivered His people from slavery and given them the Promised Land of milk and honey, but He had commissioned David's son, the third king of Israel, to build a temple in Jerusalem where sacrifices would be made and God would be worshiped.

It's important to realize, however, that Solomon ruled during one of the rare periods of Israel's history when God's people occupied their own land and enjoyed peace and secure borders. When Solomon's son Rehoboam assumed the throne after Solomon's death, a political dispute erupted. Jeroboam organized opposition to Rehoboam and succeeded in leading the northern tribes to secede and form their own kingdom. The northern kingdom of Israel and the southern kingdom of Judah then waged periodic warfare against each other, fell into idolatry, and eventually were both carried away into captivity.

I review this part of Israel's story to make a point: Most of the history of God's Old Testament people involves displacement. Abraham left his home in Ur when God called him to sojourn in a foreign land. Abraham's son Isaac, the son of promise, died before seeing God fulfill His promise of creating from Abraham a mighty nation. Then Isaac's son Jacob, the father of twelve sons, found himself and his family displaced from familiar surroundings when famine struck and they settled in Egypt.

The story of Jacob's wandering, and how he found favor in Egypt, centers on one of the Bible's grandest stories of wandering: the story of Joseph, a Hebrew dreamer who rose to second in command in all of Egypt. Let us look at his life.

THE RESTLESS DREAMER

As a young man, Joseph became an exile not by volunteering for the job, but because it was part of God's plan. Like his great-grandfather Abraham, Joseph left his home and his family and ended up in a foreign land. But unlike Abraham, Joseph was uprooted through a process of deceit fed by jealousy. And unlike his great-grandfather, Joseph did not have the benefit of God's promise that his sojourning was part of a bigger divine scheme. Joseph's wandering was forced upon him when his brothers sold him into slavery.

It's difficult for us to accept that obedience to God would lead to slavery, unjust accusations, and imprisonment. But all of those happened to Joseph, who remained uncomplaining in his obedience to God. He maintained his integrity and followed God no matter what it led to, without a blueprint that clarified his future role in God's plan to redeem His people. When we read his story in Scripture, we learn that Joseph was displaced from his home, becoming an exile in Egypt, because God needed him there.

We saw in earlier chapters that sin and rebellion created restlessness in the hearts of many Old Testament characters, such as Cain and Nimrod. In their lives the lack of contentment led to building cities and even civilizations that stood in opposition to God. But obedience to God can also result in wandering far from home. Sometimes God initiates our restlessness to see if we will follow him in obedience, even when we're not aware of God's purpose behind it. God calls us out of our comfort zones and into unexpected realms.

Joseph is one of Scripture's most dramatic examples of such wandering. When he was a teenager, Joseph had dreams of playing a prominent role both in his family and among his people. These dreams stirred a restlessness inside him, a growing awareness that someday he would be used by God. Joseph was never secretive about these dreams, and his brothers got tired of listening to the dreamer talk about his glorious future as a leader. They became jealous and conspired to kill him. Instead of killing him, however, they sold him into slavery. Thus began Joseph's restless sojourn into greatness.[3]

If we were describing the path to greatness, most of us would never include these steps: Become a slave, get thrown into prison on false charges, and hope that somehow you'll be released. But Joseph endured these injustices through year after year of devastating trials. And when the time was right, God elevated Joseph to the position of prominence he had dreamed of as a young man. Joseph became prime minister of Egypt—second in power to the pharaoh. Because of Joseph's position of authority and the dreams God sent him regarding the duration of a great famine, Joseph was able to save his family, including his grieving father, Jacob, from starvation.[4] In retrospect Joseph was able to see that it was God who had sent him to Egypt for this purpose, and not the wickedness and deception of his brothers. When his family arrived in Egypt to buy food, Joseph told them, "Do not be distressed and do not be angry with yourselves for selling me here, because it was to save lives that God sent me ahead of you.... You intended to harm me, but God intended it for good."[5]

Thus Joseph's obedience in following God into slavery, false imprisonment, and eventual greatness preserved his family, a family that grew during a four-hundred-year exile in Egypt to number some two million.

OBEDIENT WANDERING

While men occupy center stage in many of the Bible's best-known dramas, women also showed great courage in following God's command to leave the comfort of home and follow Him into a foreign land. Ruth was a Gentile woman who married the son of an Israelite who had moved his family to Moab during a famine. After the father and the son both died,

Ruth remained loyal to her widowed mother-in-law, Naomi. Ruth left her own country, forsaking her family and friends, her culture and religion, to travel with Naomi back to the older woman's home in Bethlehem.

"Don't urge me to leave you or to turn back from you," Ruth told Naomi. "Where you go I will go, and where you stay I will stay. Your people will be my people and your God my God. Where you die I will die, and there I will be buried." [6] There is no bolder statement of faith and commitment in all of Scripture.

Something inside Ruth compelled her to leave everything she'd ever known to follow after the God of her mother-in-law. Ruth, a young widow herself, was leaving behind all that was familiar to her. But her unwavering obedience to this drawing of the Holy Spirit brought her a special blessing. In Bethlehem she married Boaz, a wealthy relative of her late husband, and through their son Obed, she became an ancestor of both King David and Jesus. [7]

RESTLESSNESS THAT LEADS TO REDEMPTION

Joseph and Ruth are but two examples of people who became exiles and wanderers in response to God's call, in obedience to His command, and to further God's purpose of preserving a people for Himself. This kind of discontent, the restlessness that leads us to God and His grace, is the journey of redemption.

It is important to realize that the restlessness that God stirred in these people led not only to the redemption of the individual involved but extended to untold future generations, to an entire nation, and even to the work of God among us today. In obedience to God, Abraham left behind his extended family and his livelihood and became a homeless wanderer. It was through the obedient wandering of Abraham, a hero of faith, that God set into motion His plan of redemption for humankind.

In His sovereign grace, God revealed Himself to this descendant of Shem. Abraham, originally called Abram, was from a wealthy family in Ur, situated on the banks of the Euphrates River and the most important city in southern Mesopotamia. The ruins of ancient Ur have been located about halfway between the Persian Gulf and modern-day Baghdad.

Ur was a prosperous religious and commercial center in the ancient world and home to an advanced culture. The Babylonians worshiped many gods, but Ur was devoted to the moon god, regarded as the supreme deity. Somehow Abram remained unstained by the religious pollution of his culture, and he obediently answered the call of the one true God to pull up stakes and begin a lengthy sojourn.

When he left Mesopotamia, Abram did not know his destination. God simply told him: "Leave your country, your people and your father's household and go to the land I will show you."[8] The Lord also promised that He would make a great nation out of Abram's descendants and changed his name from Abram, meaning "exalted father," to Abraham, "father of a multitude."[9] Can you imagine encountering a God who is foreign to your own culture, hearing Him tell you to leave home for an undisclosed location, and then doing it? And once you obey that initial command, God changes your name and tells you He will make a mighty nation out of you. You want to believe this part, but you're an old man and your elderly wife has always been infertile.

Most of us would start questioning our sanity at that point, but Abraham continued to follow God no matter how irrational it seemed. Abraham's sojourn eventually brought him to a city that was destined to be dedicated to the worship of God, a city where people of all nationalities and backgrounds would come in the distant future to learn about the true God.

Abraham first encountered this city when he paid tribute to Melchizedek, the priest-king of Salem, which means "peace." Both the Psalms and the New Testament tell us that Melchizedek, whose name means "king of righteousness," was a type of Christ, our Prince of Peace and King of Righteousness.[10]

It would be almost a thousand years after Abraham first entered Salem that King David would conquer the city from the Jebusites and Jerusalem finally became the center for worship of almighty God. As we saw in the previous chapter, David is another example of a biblical character whose restlessness led to redemption.

The nation of Israel reached the height of its glory under David's leadership, but he struggled with the temptations that accompany the trappings of power and wealth. He committed adultery with the beautiful Bathsheba, and an attempt to hide that sin led him to commit another: David conspired to commit murder. The king ordered Bathsheba's husband, Uriah, to be placed on the front lines of battle where he was certain to be killed.

Like Cain, the first murderer, David committed an egregious sin. In contrast to Cain, however, when David's sin was exposed he humbled himself before God and repented. David's experience of divine forgiveness left him with an even deeper desire to honor God.[11] Think back to Cain and how he built the first city—a city in opposition to God. Because the inhabitants of Cain's city rejected God, the city of man represented human arrogance and pride. God had in mind a different kind of city, one where He would be honored and worshiped, a place where people could congregate to learn about the one true God. With Abraham, and later with David, God made provision for that city. In Jerusalem, God's name would be glorified. Jerusalem would become known as the City of God. But as glorious as this city was, it was only God's temporary provision, a mere foreshadowing of the eternal city of God that is to come.

GOD'S CITY ON EARTH

God's original plan was for humanity to dwell in a garden, where all people would have unhindered fellowship with their Creator. But the paradise of the Garden of Eden was despoiled by the sin of Adam and Eve. Then their son Cain left Eden and built a city in opposition to God. Much later we see God looking beyond man's rebellion and permitting a righteous man, the repentant David, to set aside a city that would bring glory to God. In spite of—or perhaps because of—his sin, David had a deep desire to revere God. When he repented, David expressed a longing to be in God's presence. "Create in me a pure heart," David implored the Lord, "and renew a steadfast spirit within me. Do not cast me from your presence or take your Holy Spirit from me."[12]

In a sovereign act of grace and election, the Lord honored David's desire to build Jerusalem into a center of worship. God's gracious dealings with David should inspire us all. If your deepest desire is to bring glory to God, then God will overrule the fumbling and stumbling in your life just as He did with King David. When your desire is to honor the Lord Jesus Christ, God will pour out a blessing on you.

King David authored many of the psalms, and when you read his writings it's obvious just how deeply he delighted in the presence of God. The temple musicians used many of David's psalms for public worship—and today the church still sings the psalms of David. When Solomon dedicated the temple in Jerusalem, the temple his father had dreamed of building, God's glory fell upon the worshipers.[13] Our inner discontent is often a deep hunger for God, a desire to glorify Him and to experience His glory. There is a promise of God that satisfies this restless hunger: Wherever God is honored and sought, He will show up in all His glory.

I have seen this in my own ministry. When we started The Church of the Apostles in Atlanta, we met in a school chapel. We worshiped there for six years, and God showed up. Then He showed up in the office building where we worshiped for the next seven years. And then we moved into our new sanctuary, and God showed up there. Why? Because we sought Him with all our hearts. What would happen if we failed to seek God's glory above all else, if we somehow got sidetracked by the social gospel or a watered-down gospel of entertainment? God would not be found in our midst. His Spirit would depart, and we would wither and die as a congregation.

But as much as God manifested His presence in Jerusalem, this was still only God's temporary provision. It was an earthly city inhabited by people who were far from holy. If you study the history of Jerusalem, you'll read a story that contains a fair share of bloodshed. When the people of Jerusalem quit seeking God wholeheartedly, God departed from His holy temple in His holy city. In the same way, God will depart from any church where His glory is not sought first and foremost.

A CITY WITH A CONDITIONAL BLESSING

David and Solomon offered Jerusalem to God as a sacrifice—the sacrifice Cain refused to make—and God accepted it. As long as Israel continued to seek and to worship the true God, the city would enjoy God's protection and prosperity. His presence would dwell in His city as long as His people sought Him and honored Him.

During the reigns of David and Solomon, Israel reached its highest glory, both politically and spiritually. But after Solomon died, the kingdom split and gradually the people turned away from God. When the inhabitants of Jerusalem began to worship other gods, the wicked and corrupt Babylonians were allowed to ransack Jerusalem, which fell to their hands in 586 B.C. The Babylonians looted and burned the temple and took captive many thousands of the Jewish people, whom they forced into exile.

After more than seventy years of captivity in Babylon, a remnant of the Jewish people returned to Jerusalem. Under the leadership of Zerubbabel, these Jews rebuilt their temple and rededicated their lives to God. Over time, however, their zeal for the Lord again diminished, and the spiritual vitality of the people of Jerusalem waned.

When Jesus entered Jerusalem, we see just how corrupt the keepers of the temple had become. In a burst of righteous anger, Jesus overturned the tables of the money-changers, who were charging exorbitant rates to exchange the worshipers' money into the currency of the temple treasury. Then He used a whip to drive out the merchants who were selling sheep and doves for sacrificial offerings. The money-changers and sellers had set up shop within the temple itself. "How dare you turn my Father's house into a market!" Jesus thundered at them.[14]

Finally, at the point when the city rejected its Messiah and became the place of His crucifixion, earthly Jerusalem was rejected forever as God's dwelling place. When the City of God rejected God in human flesh, the city fell from His favor, becoming instead a corrupted city of man.

Jesus lamented the city's rejection of Him. Yet He did not speak angrily to the citizens of Jerusalem. Instead, He wept hot tears because they had not recognized the day of their visitation by God. Scripture says:

> As he approached Jerusalem and saw the city, he wept over it and said, "If you, even you, had only known on this day what would bring you peace—but now it is hidden from your eyes. The days will come upon you when your enemies will build an embankment against you and encircle you and hem you in on every side. They will dash you to the ground, you and the children within your walls. They will not leave one stone on another, because you did not recognize the time of God's coming to you."[15]

In A.D. 70 the armies of Rome leveled the temple, fulfilling the prophecy of Christ, and the glorious temple that once served as the center of worship to God has never been rebuilt. Only a portion of one wall remains standing, and although the Jews again occupy Jerusalem, the Temple Mount is under the control of Muslim religious authorities. Jesus had seen this destruction coming, and He wept over Jerusalem.

I believe God is weeping over America today. The Founding Fathers sought to set up a biblical model of government, a system of laws that honor God and provide protection and prosperity for a free people. But today in America, God is rejected. His Spirit is quenched, and His presence is not sought.

I believe God is also weeping over the church. Godly men, like John Knox, John Wesley, and a host of others, founded denominations to lift up the name of Jesus. Now many in the mainline denominations that grew from the work of these great men deny the divinity of Christ, and God's presence has departed from their midst.

A SHADOW OF THE HEAVENLY JERUSALEM

Earthly Jerusalem and its temple were only a dim representation of what it means for God to indwell the praises of His people, a rough sketch of what can happen when the glory of God is fully revealed.

Ezekiel tells us that in the heavenly Jerusalem we will truly understand what it means to say Yahweh-Shammah—"THE LORD IS THERE."[16] But like earthly Jerusalem, we cannot fully comprehend what it means for God to be with us all the time. Why? Because on earth our discontent often leads us to run away from Him. We tend to forget His commandments and close our ears to His voice. Instead, we are seduced by the voices and the standards of the world system.

In the heavenly Jerusalem, however, we will have unending communion with God. There will be no television or Internet to divert our attention. No one to whisper doubts and fear and anxiety in our ears, for God's righteousness will be permanently with us.

In the earthly Jerusalem, God's presence was sporadic. He showed up when His people lifted His name high. But in the New Jerusalem, He will always be there because His name will constantly be lifted high. In earthly Jerusalem, God's blessings were conditional. But in the Jerusalem to come, His unconditional blessing will be fulfilled and true believers will worship Him forever. People will no longer seek after worldly pleasures but will delight themselves in the Lord.

In the New Jerusalem we will experience uninterrupted fellowship with God, just as Adam and Eve enjoyed His presence in the garden. In the meantime, as we look ahead to the New Jerusalem, we can have intimacy with the God who longs to fellowship with us here on earth. When our discontent springs from a burning hunger for God, we will seek Him with our whole hearts and He will allow us to find Him.

DISCOVERING THE PLACE OF REST

Today, more than any other time in Christian history, the word *grace* is no longer amazing. Most Americans are familiar with the hymn "Amazing Grace," but few have really understood the concept of God's grace.

Yet the Bible is replete with word pictures that teach us about God's grace by describing His constant wooing of His wandering children. There is perhaps no more powerful depiction of God's amazing grace than the story of the prodigal son. In this story we witness the repentant return of a wayward son into the arms of a grace-filled father. This is a true picture of God's grace—the one place where discontent begins to fade.

In this section, we'll examine some of the many ways in which God has taken the initiative to quench our thirst and to answer our longing. This is the grace of God that finally brings an end to our restlessness.

Six

COMING HOME
TO THE GOD OF GRACE

Even in Our Rebellious Wandering, God Can Find Us

Jashub woke up in a narrow alley behind Merchant's Street. He was stiff from sleeping on cobblestones. The pavement had become his bed when he lost his quarters in the residential district; the landlord had kicked him out when he could no longer pay the rent. His money was gone and so were his friends. They left when the wine stopped flowing.

The young man shook himself awake and ran his fingers through his matted hair. Time to get moving, before the vendors arrived and opened their stalls. Perhaps the arthritic old man who sold dates and almonds would pay Jashub a few coins again for sweeping out his stall and setting up the canopy. If the kindly old man failed to show up, Jashub would offer to work for other vendors. He had come to the city flush with money and drunk on dreams of an easy life with new friends. Now he was alone and sleeping on the ground, dependent on the whims of shopkeepers for a few coins to buy bread.

When the elderly shopkeeper failed to arrive, Jashub swallowed his pride and went to the gruff merchant in the next stall. "I'll work for food," he told the seller of rugs. "That's all I ask, just something to eat."

"Don't you know there's a famine in the land?" came the reply. "I don't make enough profit to feed my own family, let alone some filthy vagrant."

Jashub walked away in shame. He was exhausted, he was hungry, and yes, he was filthy. For the first time in many months, he thought of home and longed to be there. He'd been so eager to take his inheritance and make his own way in the world. But in his father's house he'd had whatever he needed—good food, a warm bed, regular work, and sturdy leather sandals. He looked down at his feet, tender from walking barefoot like a slave. He had traded his sandals for the last complete meal he had eaten.

Standing at the edge of the marketplace, Jashub realized he had nothing left to sell. Would he have to steal in order to feed himself?

Suddenly a stocky man walked up and asked Jashub if he was looking for work.

"Yes sir," the young man responded.

"Do you know anything about animals?"

"My father has large herds of cattle and sheep. I'm very familiar with his business." Jashub stood straighter as the man looked him up and down, probably wondering why a landowner's son was so dirty and disheveled.

The man finally nodded and said, "Come with me."

Jashub eagerly followed the man, struggling to keep up. After several miles of walking, his feet were raw and throbbing. But there was no time for rest. When they arrived at their destination and the farmer put Jashub to work, the young man immediately regretted his decision to take this job. The man had no cattle or sheep, only pigs. His job was to feed unclean animals he would never have touched if he hadn't been starving. But he was starving, so as Jashub scattered carob pods to feed the swine, he longed to fill his stomach with those same pods. He had squandered his inheritance and now he was starving while these vile pigs inhaled seed pods he would gladly have eaten.

No one offered Jashub any food, and when he lay down on some straw in the barn that night, his empty stomach kept him awake. As darkness fell, he couldn't keep his mind from wandering back to his father's estate. The hired men there went to sleep every night with a full stomach. In fact, they had food to spare. He would go back and beg his father's mercy. He knew that his father might turn him away. But he would risk his father's rejection, hoping that he might at least be accepted as a servant.

Before daylight broke, Jashub went to the trough and splashed water on his face. He would make himself as presentable as he could for the long journey. He would tell his father that he knew he had sinned against heaven and against him. "I'm not worthy to be your son," he would say. "Treat me like one of your hired men."

For days Jashub walked toward home on scarred feet. His food consisted of grass and berries, and once he was fortunate to dine on the scraps of food left behind by a departing caravan.

Relief flooded over him when he passed by the city closest to his father's estate. Only two more miles and he would be home. His relief turned to apprehension, however, as he tried to picture the reception that awaited him. It could be no reception at all, but cold rejection.

While he was still some distance from the estate, he saw a figure running toward him. Jashub froze. Did the man mean to harm him? Before he could decide whether to flee, he realized that it was his father. The old man was shouting, "Praise be to God! Oh, Jashub, my son! Praise be to God!"

Exhaustion overcame the tired traveler when his father rushed up and threw his arms around him. Jashub collapsed against his father and began to weep. The old man kissed his son, still praising God and saying, "My son, my son."

"Father, I have sinned against heaven and against you," Jashub said in a tremulous voice. "I am no longer worthy to be called your son."[1]

The father called to the servants who had followed him out to meet the returning son. "Fetch the best robe for Jashub. Put sandals on his feet and my signet ring on his finger. Kill a calf and prepare for a feast. We must celebrate, for this son of mine was dead and is alive again."[2]

As the servants helped the hungry, exhausted Jashub toward the house, he could hear his father weeping and shouting, "My son has come home!" Jashub's stomach was empty, but his heart was full of joy because he had received his father's forgiveness and because his wandering was finally over.

⌒

The prodigal son in Jesus' story gives us a gripping portrait of a person who deliberately wanders away from God in pride and ingratitude. Unlike Joseph, Abraham, or Ruth, whose sojourns began in obedience to God's call or through His intervention, the prodigal son left home out of willfulness. He insisted on getting what was his and then he left, turning his back on his father.

The first part of this story is tragic, as the loving father watches his son's figure grow smaller and smaller and then disappear in the distance. But the son eventually reaches a turning point, and the story has a joyous ending. Unlike Cain and Nimrod, who rebelled against God and refused to repent and turn back to Him, the prodigal son ended his sinful wandering when he reached the end of himself. It was then that he recalled his father's love and care, and he returned home as a broken, repentant son.

If you have trouble relating to biblical heroes and heroines such as Abraham and Ruth, then think of your life in comparison to that of the prodigal son. He was no hero, simply an ordinary person. He accomplished no great feats, he showed no great courage, and he was not a great leader. Neither did he live a life of practiced obedience. But he did remember his father when his wandering fed him the bitter fruit that comes from disobedience. We saw in chapter 4 that David's suffering heightened his reliance on God, but David's despair came as a result of his son's murderous plotting, not because of his own rebellion. Most of us can identify more easily with the prodigal son, who brought despair and humiliation on himself.

Like this young man, we find ourselves wandering far from the Father who loves us. Often we recognize that we're putting distance between ourselves and God, but still we continue on our way. The glorious news in Scripture is that while we experiment with life apart from God, He patiently waits for His wandering children to return. And He welcomes us home with the joy and warm embrace we see in this story.

THE DEEPER MEANING OF GRACE

The behavior of the younger son, who demanded his share of the inheritance and squandered it in immoral living, sets up a perfect scene for the demonstration of his father's grace. The son, asserting his rights, journeyed to a faraway country, leaving the security of home to chase an elusive dream of self-fulfillment. His wandering brought him the momentary pleasures of a life of excess, but it also left him debased and humiliated.

Finally he came to the end of himself and faced a different type of discontent. Whereas his former restlessness had led only to a place of hunger, shame, and poverty, a new kind of restlessness would take him back home where he would find grace. His loving father had been patiently waiting and hoping for the return of the ungrateful, wandering rebel.

It is difficult to read this story without getting a lump in your throat, so beautiful is the portrait of the loving father who runs to embrace his returning son. The story is a dramatic portrayal of God's undeserved grace. The free gift of God's grace goes against every human instinct and every other religious system in the world. The Buddhist eightfold path, the Hindu doctrine of karma, the Jewish ceremonial law, and the Islamic *sharia* law are comprised of ways for followers of those religions to earn divine approval. Only Jesus Christ, the eternal Son of God, through whom the world was created, offers unconditional love. Only God in human flesh could be so extravagant in His generosity.

But why would God continue to offer us His free gift of grace, especially after we willfully rebel and wander far from Him, rejecting His love and resisting His efforts to woo us back? God's nature won't allow Him to do anything other than to pursue those who are lost, those who are wandering in disobedience, those who desperately need Him but who have not yet recognized that He is missing from their lives. Many in our society are more interested in exercising their rights than they are in being humbled by God's undeserved grace. In a world with civil rights, animal rights, and gay rights, grace hardly seems necessary. The gospel of political correctness reigns supreme, and many confuse grace with being nice. Most people believe they can be good on their own, without relying on God's grace.

We recognize the inner discontent, the continuing search for a better life, for peace and fulfillment. But we fail to see that the solution to this restlessness is found in God and His grace.

Since grace is easily ignored and even discounted, let's take a careful look at what it is and how it holds the power to change our discontented heart. Scripture describes two types of grace. The first is what theologians refer to as "common grace," but more accurately it should be called "mercy," which is freely given to everyone. For example, Jesus told us that God "causes his sun to rise on the evil and the good, and sends rain on the righteous and the unrighteous."[3] The beauty of God's creation is free for everyone to enjoy, whether they follow God or not.

In contrast to God's mercy, however, His grace is exclusively given to those who belong to Christ. This grace is uniquely lavished upon those who have accepted the sacrifice of God's Son and received Him as their Savior and Lord. This grace is the unmerited favor of God, and it is irresistible and inexhaustible. This is the grace that satisfies our longing for peace and ultimate contentment.

As we seek to understand grace, we also need to draw a distinction between the God of grace and the grace of God. God is infinite, but His grace is not. God is eternal; He has no end. But His grace will one day cease, and His judgment will take over.

It's difficult to convey the graciousness of God to a generation that believes the world owes it something. As a communicator of God's truth and a teacher of His Word, I am well aware of the challenge. Nonetheless, to constantly revel in the God of grace and the grace of God is the most exhilarating aspect of the Christian life.

The God of Grace

The God of grace can radically change your life, and He wants to do just that. Remember how God approached the first couple in the Garden of Eden after they violated His one prohibition. What happened in the Garden of Eden between God and Adam and Eve affects us every day through our inherited sin nature. So it's vitally important that we consider the affects on our own lives.

Adam and Eve were offended by God's command when he told them, "If you eat from the tree, you will die."[4] But the serpent said, in essence, "If you eat from the tree, you will live."[5] Eve rejected the word of the God of truth and subjected the matter to her own judgment.

That same tendency to elevate our own reason above God's clear command characterizes our times. We like to say, "I'll be the judge of that." But when it comes to issues clearly spelled out in Scripture, if you try to decide a matter for yourself, you will surely go the wrong way.

Eve decided to put the forbidden fruit to a pragmatic test. "I just want to check its nutritional value." She put it under an aesthetic test. "Would it look nice in the living room?" Then she put the fruit to an intellectual test. "Will I learn something new from eating it?" Needless to say, the fruit passed all these tests. So Eve decided that the devil was right, and she shared the news with her husband, so he also ate the fruit.

This scene is repeated millions of times each day. People go through the same thought process. *If God were really good, He wouldn't forbid me to do something I want to do. If I abide by all of God's prohibitions, then I won't be fulfilled in life. Since the Bible contradicts so many of my desires, it must be wrong.*

Adam and Eve's temptation is the same temptation we face today— whether to believe God's Word and obey it. Their disobedience and fall from grace is a true picture of the state of all human beings. But whether we acknowledge it or not, God is in charge. This is His universe, and His justice demands that sin be judged.

Sin is tragic, but it does give us a vivid contrast between God's way and our willful way. It provides a dark backdrop against which we can contrast the death of sin and the life that comes by God's grace. Whereas Satan caused doubt in Eve's mind by calling into question what God had commanded, God remained true when He manifested His life-giving grace to Adam and Eve.

We see the goodness of God's grace in three ways:

1. They Did Not Immediately Die

Adam and Eve did die spiritually—but not physically—as soon as they ate the fruit. The evidence of their spiritual demise is that they hid from God after they sinned. God had said that the day they ate from the tree, they would die. That's justice. "Do the crime, then do the time," we say today.

But then the God of grace comes and says, "I will give you an opportunity to repent." That's the first way God demonstrated His grace. Adam and Eve's earthly lives continued so they could repent and once again draw near to God. And amazingly, the God of grace did even more. He gave them hope to believe in the Savior that would be coming to the world.[6]

2. They Were Promised a Redeemer

God told Adam and Eve that a Redeemer would come to undo Satan's deception. Genesis 3:15 is the first announcement of the gospel of Jesus Christ. At the time Adam and Eve did not comprehend all that God was saying, but they understood enough to know that a Redeemer was coming. It took thousands of years before the promised Redeemer was announced to Mary and Joseph by the angel Gabriel, who instructed them to name the child Jesus, because He would save His people from their sins.

3. They Were Given Salvation

The God of grace brought salvation to our first parents. The Lord made garments of skin for them and clothed them.[7] For God to provide that, Adam and Eve had to witness the first slaying of an innocent animal to cover their shame. Thus their first lesson in grace was that an innocent must die for the guilty. In Genesis 3 we see the first biblical glimmer of understanding that the sinless, innocent Son of God would someday die for guilty sinners.

The Bible makes it clear that every human is born with Adam and Eve's sin genes. Just as we inherit our ancestors' physical genes, we also inherit Adam and Eve's spiritual genes. Those genes are manifested in the way our pride rules supreme and in our tendency to disobey and rebel against God.

In his epistle to the Ephesians, Paul shows how we are rescued from the effects of these sin genes. God's justice system declares that if our sin genes are not dealt with, the consequences are eternal punishment. The court of heaven demands that if we break God's laws—and because of original sin, it's inevitable that we will—then we will have a dismal future of utter loneliness and bleak darkness, eternally separated from God.

But God has provided a remedy, a way for us to overcome those sin genes and to be free of them forever. Some people agree that our sin genes have consequences, but they think that the way to deal with them is to do good works, hoping that their charitable deeds will balance out the effects of sin. But this is not God's way. We can do nothing good apart from God, and no matter how much good we end up doing, it can never pay for our sins. The Bible tells us that no one can ascend to God's dwelling place based on his own merits. No one can earn God's favor or buy his way into heaven. It is impossible for us to get to God through our own efforts.

Biblical Christianity teaches that God has come to us! That's what is amazing about grace, and it is what sets Christian faith apart from other religious systems. God came to us in the person of Jesus Christ, and it is only through Him that we can come to God. It's like the child's description of an elevator: "I got into this little room, and the upstairs came down." We cannot enter God's chamber uninvited. We can only meet Him when He comes down to us.

The Grace of God

In the second chapter of Ephesians, Paul summarized the way in which God comes to us through His Son, the Lord Jesus Christ. As we examine these verses, we will see that Paul wrote about three things that we need to understand about God's grace in the life of a Christian.

1. We Are Rescued from a Dismal Past

Because of our inherited sin genes, we are born spiritually dead. Things don't get more dismal than that. "As for you, you were dead in your transgressions and sins, in which you used to live when you followed the ways of this world and of the ruler of the kingdom of the air, the spirit who is now at work in those who are disobedient."[8]

Some people think there's nothing wrong with the human race that science and technology cannot cure. But science and technology have discovered far more diseases than they have eliminated. Science and technology have never managed to eradicate poverty. And science and technology cannot overcome the ultimate challenge—death.

Others recognize that without God we have no hope of spiritual life and salvation. But they erroneously assume that part of the credit goes to them. They compare their inherent sinfulness to being in a ditch. "I could not climb out by myself," they claim, "but then Jesus came and took my hand, and He pulled me out." That is absolutely incorrect. The Bible says that before we encountered Christ, we were dead in sin. How can a dead person stretch out his hand? How can a dead person even know that he's in a ditch?

Before God's grace came into our lives, we were spiritual corpses! It was impossible for us to make a move toward God. But while we were spiritually dead, we were physically alive, up and about, and actively proclaiming our independence from God. As Paul described it, we were like dead men walking. Not only were we dead, but we were also enslaved to sin, obeying "the ruler of the kingdom of the air." We were slaves of Satan.

Prior to encountering the God of grace, we were filled with greed, hatred, lust, arrogance, and self-assertion. We had no room for God. And because we were enslaved to Satan and the world's system, we were subject to God's wrath.

Whoa! That word *wrath* tends to set people on edge. Anybody who utters the term is called angry and hateful. But let me direct you back to God's Word. Ephesians 2:3 says, "All of us also lived among them [the disobedient] at one time, gratifying the cravings of our sinful nature and following its desires and thoughts. Like the rest, we were by nature objects of wrath."

Yes, God is loving and merciful. But He is a God of wrath when it comes to sin. Those who don't know God fail to take His wrath seriously because they don't take sin seriously. How can they? They're spiritually dead.

In contrast, Christians have no reason to fear God's wrath. If you have received salvation through the grace of God, then you will never be under wrath again. However, if you have never received God's grace, you are still, because of your sin nature, an object of His wrath. But you can change your status in the briefest of moments. Perhaps you were led to pick up this book just so God could show you His grace. You can meet the God of grace right now—even before you finish reading this chapter—and you can override those inherited sin genes instantly. It sounds unbelievable, but it's true. You can be transformed, and you can change your spiritual address from the kingdom of darkness to the kingdom of God's glorious light.

Are you ready to receive God's grace? Then turn to the back of this book where you'll find a sample prayer to guide you. (See Appendix A: "A Prayer to Receive Eternal Security Through Jesus Christ"). Perhaps you have received God's grace, but your restless heart has caused you to wander away from Him. There's another prayer in the back of this book for you, a prayer that will help you return home to the heart of God. (See Appendix B: "A Prayer to Renew Your Commitment to Jesus Christ").

Go ahead and pray, I'll wait on you…

Now that God's grace has taken away your dismal past, let's look at the glorious present God has prepared for you.

2. He Gives Us a Glorious Present Every Day

The Christian's past is a dreadful condition—a shameful state of "disgrace"—but when God's grace comes in, everything is changed. Here's what Paul said about this transformation: "But because of his great love for us, God, who is rich in mercy, made us alive with Christ even when we were dead in transgressions—it is by grace you have been saved. And God raised us up with Christ and seated us with him in the heavenly realms in Christ Jesus."[9]

What a radical change! You're no longer a "dead man walking"; you're alive in Christ! You have been saved by God's grace and lifted up to the heavenly realms with Christ Jesus. You have been set free from the power and the consequences of sin. God has performed "gene therapy" on you, removing the harmful effects of your inherited sin genes.

You were once enslaved to sin, but now you are free. There are no slaves in heaven, and that's where you are seated right now—in the heavenly realm. If you are the recipient of God's grace, you can have victory over lust, greed, anger, jealousy, envy, fear, anxiety, doubt. You can have victory over addiction to alcohol, pornography, drugs.

When grace comes in, God's power comes in with it. When you trusted Christ as your Savior, the chains that bound you to Satan's kingdom were broken and you were set free. If you are still enslaved to sin, then either you don't know you've been set free or you never learned how to claim your victory.

The Bible says you are *already* seated in heavenly places.[10] Not some time down the road, when your earthly life comes to an end. No, right now you are seated in heavenly places because you have been marvelously saved by God's grace.

To live in grace, we must constantly keep in mind that we are saved by God's grace. We don't contribute anything to the process: "For it is by grace you have been saved, through faith—and this not from yourselves, it is the gift of God—not by works, so that no one can boast."[11] Salvation is the gift of God, and it is received by faith. But understand something about the faith that leads us into salvation: It is God's gift to you, a gift of

His grace. People think faith is something you have to generate from within. We're always trying to work up more faith. But it is impossible to generate something that comes only as a gift from God.

When we exercise faith in believing and receiving God's gift of eternal life, we are exercising faith that God gave us. It wasn't faith that we somehow unearthed from deep within ourselves. God gave it to us. Otherwise you could take credit for working up enough faith to accept God's grace, and you cannot be saved by your merits.

3. He Gives Us an Incredible Future

The grace of God not only takes away our dismal past and gives us a glorious present, but it gives us two glorious futures that are as bright as God Himself. I wrote *futures* in the plural because there is an immediate future of God's favor and blessing, and then there is the distant future.

Our immediate future consists of being ambassadors of the King of kings. An ambassador does not live according to the way he or she feels. Rather, an ambassador represents the government of his home country. In the same way, those who are saved by grace are God's ambassadors. We do what He wants us to do and say what He wants us to say.[12]

These are the "good works" Paul writes about in Ephesians 2:10: "For we are God's workmanship, created in Christ Jesus to do good works, which God prepared in advance for us to do."

Our good works do not save us, but once we are saved we can be confident that God has good works in store for us. Scripture shows that God already has a plan for us as ambassadors. Even before we received His salvation, Paul said, God was planning these works for us in advance.

God brought you into His kingdom with a specific mission in mind. It may not be glamorous. In fact, it might be tedious and lowly. But there is a work He wants you to do in gratitude for what He has done. Ministry does not just mean preaching or teaching or leading praise and worship. A ministry of good works could be taking food to a neighbor, visiting a lonely person in a nursing home, or speaking a kind word to a harried store clerk.

These good works are the immediate future God has for us, but Paul also tells us about our distant future. God has seated us in the heavenly realms, Paul wrote, "in order that in the coming ages he might show the incomparable riches of his grace, expressed in his kindness to us in Christ Jesus."[13] Even if we run full speed away from God like a prodigal son or daughter, His grace compels Him to open His arms to receive us when we come to the end of ourselves. God rescues us from the destruction of our sin, and He does this even though we are entirely undeserving of His grace. God takes the initiative to quench our thirst, to answer our longing for contentment, and to put an end to our restlessness. Just like the prodigal son, we can be an ungrateful son or daughter who wanders far from God, only to realize our deep need and turn, run back, and be caught up in the arms of our grace-filled Father. In God's grace, we find that our discontent begins to fade. In the embrace of God, we find peace and rest for our souls.

God has lavished His grace on us here and now, but He will completely overwhelm us with His grace in the hereafter. Nothing we experience on earth can compare to the blessings He will bestow on us in the life to come. Thus our immediate future on earth can be one of peace and fulfillment because of God's grace and the good works He has prepared for us. And our eternal future will be one of unending joy, worship, and enjoyment of God, because His grace is the only thing that secures our salvation.

The end of our discontent can begin on earth as we accept the free gift of God's grace. And in the life to come, we will experience the final answer to our search for rest. Earthly discontent disappears in the presence of God.

Part 4

DETOURS ON THE PATH TO GOD

In the previous chapters we looked at the loss of contentment, tracing its effects in the lives of several biblical figures. And as we saw in chapter 6, even the type of discontent that leads a person away from God can reach a turning point, when wandering becomes the path back to God.

As we fall gladly into God's welcoming arms and set our feet on a new path, we need to be aware of attitudes, habits, and circumstances that can send us off course. If we're not aware of these detours, we'll lose the peace and contentment that come from God. Accepting God's grace and receiving forgiveness for our sins initiates our sojourn to the heart of God. Once we're on that path, however, we need to avoid the dangerous detours.

Before you turn the page, let me point out that the following chapters are written to those who have found rest for their souls in Christ. If you have not yet decided to accept Jesus Christ as your personal Savior, you can do so today. Simply turn to the back of this book and use the prayer in Appendix A to begin a relationship with the only One who can grant you rest, peace, and eternal life.

Seven

CONFRONTING OUR WEAKNESSES

Satan's Strategy for Distracting Those Who Follow God

The driver of the beat-up Volkswagen Beetle edged into the passing lane to see if he could pull around the lumbering truck ahead, then quickly jerked the car back into his lane when he saw the oncoming traffic. He sighed and slapped the steering wheel with the heel of his hand. The six-hundred-mile drive to Melbourne was turning into a six-hundred-mile crawl. Every time the driver came to a straight stretch of highway and tried to pass the semi, another vehicle would appear from the opposite direction.

His passenger asked again, "Michael, would you like me to drive?"

"No, I'm fine." He wasn't being fully honest. Driving behind a truck was frustrating, and his wife's repeated offers to drive just about pushed him over the edge. Elizabeth had been sitting silently, praying with white-knuckled fervor. At least Michael suspected that was what his wife was doing. Every now and then he caught a slight movement of her lips, then a few moments later she would ask again if he wanted her to drive.

Maybe if he'd been driving a bigger, more powerful car, he could have sped around the semi. But since the young husband was a student, the 1965 VW was all he could afford. The tiny four-seater was eight years old and had seen far better days, but at least it was reliable transportation for getting around Sydney, where Michael was in seminary. On the highway it was another story.

Hume Highway. Quite an ambitious name for the winding, two-lane road that served as the main thoroughfare between the two major cities on the southeastern coast of Australia.

After another unsuccessful attempt to pass, Michael exploded in frustration. "The geniuses who spent fifteen years building that funny-looking opera house should have spent the money to build a real highway instead."

"I think the opera house is beautiful," Elizabeth said evenly. "It looks like white sails billowing out over the harbor."

Exercising discernment, Michael did not reply.

Another straight stretch of road. Another attempt to pass. Another swerve back into the left lane—the driving lane in Australia.

"Honey, if you want me to drive…"

Michael frowned at his wife. "I'm not going to get us killed, if that's what you're worried about. I just want to get there before Jesus returns." Instantly contrite over his outburst, he muttered, "I'm sorry."

He had been married to Elizabeth, a red-haired, blue-eyed beauty, for almost two years. God had provided the perfect wife for him, and Michael had never been happier. Well, except for the frustration caused by the lumbering turtle of a truck in front of them. They had picked up the semi about the time they crossed over the river at Canberra, halfway to their destination. The hills around the capital city were lush and green, but Michael was too frustrated to enjoy the scenery.

After a few more tense minutes, he edged into the right lane yet again. Finally, there was no oncoming traffic, so he gunned the engine and pulled around the truck. He was starting to smile over his apparent victory when a truck popped over the ridge ahead, straight in front of the accelerating Volkswagen. Michael's smile vanished as he shifted into second gear and slammed the accelerator to the floor. Elizabeth began to pray out loud. Michael had never pushed the car to its limit before, and his heart leaped as he felt the Beetle surge forward with a rush of power that he didn't know the forty-horsepower engine possessed.

The old Bug glided past the semi and returned safely to the left lane. They had many miles left to drive, and neither occupant had much to say.

⟿

My family and most of my parishioners in Atlanta would quickly identify me as the impatient seminary student driving the 1965 VW Beetle. Although my temperament has matured considerably in the thirty years since that episode, even now I couldn't be described as having great patience. I'm the kind of person who is constantly on the go, and I want to get where I'm going without delay.

I shared this story with you to illustrate that God's grace includes a rich reserve of supernatural power for times of spiritual emergency—times when we encounter circumstances or attitudes that could detour us away from God's grace. As I think back, that extra surge of power from my little VW Bug is, in a spiritual sense, comparable to the promise God made to the apostle Paul: "My grace is sufficient for you, for My strength is made perfect in weakness."[1]

This may sound like a contradiction. How can strength be made perfect in weakness? The Lord is telling us that we all go through times when we're trying to move ahead in life, but just as we pull into the passing lane to get around the eighteen-wheeler, another truck comes roaring down the highway from the opposite direction. If we look only at our circumstances, all we'll see are the delays, the obstacles, and the truck bearing down on us. We're just trying to make progress, but we're staring imminent danger right in the eyes—or right in the headlights, as the case may be.

At some point, we're all battered by the desperation of life's pain and loss. It might be the loss of a loved one, the loss of a job, a doctor's terrifying diagnosis, rejection by a spouse or family member, or the betrayal of a friend. Whenever these threats are barreling down the road, headed straight toward us, we can do one of two things: We can panic and rely on our own resources to escape the threat, or we can admit our weakness and helplessness and draw upon the outpouring of God's grace.

We most readily perceive our need for God when we are the weakest. When we reach the lowest point in life, we are most apt to urgently seek God in prayer. The weaker we become, the more we pray. And the more we pray, the more God's strength is made perfect in our weakness.

Threats and dangers confront all believers—from the most gifted leaders to those who are brand-new to the faith. The apostle Paul faced the threatening rush of human weakness and begged God to remove the weakness. This was a man who met Jesus in a blinding light, a man who had received visions and revelations from God. But he refused to boast about his supernatural encounters with the Lord. Instead, he boasted about his infirmities.

> To keep me from becoming conceited because of these surpass-
> ingly great revelations, there was given me a thorn in my flesh, a
> messenger of Satan, to torment me. Three times I pleaded with the
> Lord to take it away from me. But he said to me, "My grace is suf-
> ficient for you, for my power is made perfect in weakness." There-
> fore I will boast all the more gladly about my weaknesses, so that
> Christ's power may rest on me. That is why, for Christ's sake, I
> delight in weaknesses, in insults, in hardships, in persecutions, in
> difficulties. For when I am weak, then I am strong.[2]

It's interesting that Paul compares the source of his torment to a thorn. A thorn is a common thing, a small thing—not a life-threatening affliction. Still, even a small thorn can cause an enormous amount of pain. And if it is not removed, a thorn can fester and produce infection.

Thorns have been in abundant supply since Adam and Eve were banished from the garden. As God pronounced judgment on Adam's sin, He told Adam that the ground would produce thorns and thistles, making it difficult for the man to cultivate the land.

God was referring to literal thorns that would make it difficult to grow food to sustain life on earth. Writing to the Corinthians, Paul referred figuratively to a "thorn in my flesh," a constant reminder of his human frailty and limitations. Bible commentators have speculated about the nature of Paul's weakness. Some say that because he mentioned the flesh, it must have been a weakness in his moral character. John Calvin held that view.

Others have presumed that Paul picked up malaria in the mosquito-infested swamps of coastal Asia Minor, or perhaps he suffered from epilepsy. Still others have said that Paul's thorn must have been a speech impediment, inferring that condition because the apostle once said that he did not speak with eloquence.[3]

One of the more plausible explanations is that Paul had a serious eye infection that restricted his sight and caused him a great deal of embarrassment. At the end of his epistle to the Galatians, which had been dictated to a scribe, Paul picked up the pen and finished the letter himself, saying, "See what large letters I use as I write to you with my own hand!"[4] It's possible that poor eyesight necessitated Paul's writing in very large letters.

Whatever Paul's thorn was, we know it was no minor irritation. This thorn caused physical torment. We also know that the thorn was given to him during a period when he was already experiencing horrendous sufferings. He had been imprisoned and repeatedly exposed to death. But that's not all.

Five times I received from the Jews the forty lashes minus one. Three times I was beaten with rods, once I was stoned, three times I was shipwrecked, I spent a night and a day in the open sea, I have been constantly on the move. I have been in danger from rivers, in danger from bandits, in danger from my own countrymen, in danger from Gentiles; in danger in the city, in danger in the country, in danger at sea; and in danger from false brothers. I have labored and toiled and have often gone without sleep; I have known hunger and thirst and have often gone without food; I have been cold and naked. Besides everything else, I face daily the pressure of my concern for all the churches.[5]

What is significant about this catalog of trials is that Paul never asked to be delivered from any of these situations. Yet when he mentioned his thorn in the flesh, Paul acknowledged that he had pleaded with God to remove it. In light of the apostle's other ordeals, this thorn must have been a serious affliction indeed to merit such urgent prayer.

It is no accident that God the Holy Spirit, who authored the Scriptures, did not specify what Paul's problem was. The omission makes sense, since all of us who go through any form of suffering can identify with the apostle's affliction. If we had known for sure that it was poor eyesight, then only those who suffer from vision problems would have identified with Paul's struggle. By not knowing the exact nature of his suffering, we can all imagine Paul hurting with whatever hurts us. We also readily identify with Paul's prayer for the thorn to be removed.

PRAYING FOR DELIVERANCE

As he prayed, Paul quietly asked the Lord to intervene and deliver him quickly. He probably prayed the same prayer you and I have often prayed:

"Dear God, please take it away, and do it now." After a period of fervent prayer, Paul finally received an answer. But it wasn't the answer he was hoping for. Instead, the Lord told the apostle, "My grace is sufficient for you."

God's promise for you is the same. Whatever your hurt may be… whatever your pain feels like…whatever grief is crushing you—His grace is sufficient for you! His grace will give you the strength to persevere and the power to overcome.

Charles Spurgeon, one of England's greatest preachers, on numerous occasions experienced the sufficiency of God's grace. "I have oftentimes looked gratefully back to my sick chamber," he once said. "I am certain that I never did grow in grace one half so much anywhere as I have upon the bed of pain."[6]

Recently an acquaintance of mine was injured in an automobile accident. Laurie has suffered from rheumatoid arthritis since she was a young child, so an injury that would be relatively minor for anyone else can cause her immense suffering. When her car's air bag deployed, it broke Laurie's elbow and two bones in her hand. She also suffered a whiplash injury to her neck. The injuries were not life threatening, but they were quite painful nevertheless.

The next day she recounted the ordeal for a visitor. "I told the paramedics that my neck was fused from the arthritis and my legs don't straighten all the way, so I didn't want them to put me on a backboard when they pulled me out of the car. But they had to immobilize me, for my safety. The cervical collar wouldn't fit around my neck because it was too big. So they put a towel under my chin and secured my head to the backboard with surgical tape. Then they put a towel under my knees and strapped my legs down. They tried to make me as comfortable as possible, but the ambulance ride was a nightmare."

In the emergency room Laurie remained strapped in one position for three hours, which was agonizing for her stiff joints. "I begged the doctor to give me something for the pain," she said, "and before they x-rayed me, he finally ordered a shot of morphine."

Laurie's eyes filled with tears at that point. "I kept saying that the pain was excruciating. Later I got to thinking about that word, *excruciating,* which comes from the Latin word that means 'to crucify.' I thought how the crucifixion subjected the Lord to a kind of pain I can't even imagine. All I had to endure was a few broken bones and being strapped to a backboard for three hours. Jesus was nailed to a cross and shed His blood for me. *His* pain was excruciating; mine wasn't."

Thinking of the cross of Christ helped Laurie endure her suffering. She found that God's grace was sufficient even in her time of desperate need.

AVOIDING THE DETOURS

As you confront the thorns in your life, keep in mind their potential to detour you from the path of finding contentment in God. Even those who are pursuing the peace that comes from God's grace can get tripped up when they encounter painful circumstances.

To avoid the detours, keep in mind the following three biblical truths. This wisdom from Scripture will help you trust God for strength when the pain becomes intense and you are tempted to rely on your own resources rather than God's grace.

1. Satan Is the Manufacturer of Thorns

Paul described his thorn as "a messenger of Satan" that had been sent to torment him.[7] Satan never sends you love messages or gives you good news; Satan's messages, and the vehicles he uses as his messengers, will always put dread in your heart.

Identifying the source helps us put our thorns in perspective and makes us more understanding toward those who are facing difficulties. When a person is suffering through no fault of his own, the cruelest thing you can do is to behave like one of Job's "comforters." A good portion of the book of Job recounts the accusations and sermonizing of Job's supposed friends, who kept insisting that his problems were his own fault. Their advice boiled down to: "You must have a secret sin tucked away somewhere or you wouldn't be going through all these trials."

Job protested that he had searched his heart and was confident that he had not sinned against God. (I imagine Job had already confessed sins he hadn't even committed by that point.) The Bible confirms that sin had not caused Job's suffering. So why had so many calamities arrived on his doorstep? God had allowed Satan to test Job, a fact the book of Job makes clear from the first chapter.

Job understood that Satan was the manufacturer of thorns. Over and over his friends urged Job to curse God, but "in all this, Job did not sin by charging God with wrongdoing."[8]

In contrast to Job's failed comforters, who insisted that suffering was always the result of sin, there are those today who will tell you to pretend that everything is all right. In other words, refuse to admit that you have a problem, and it will simply disappear! These people act as if circumstances are real only if you acknowledge them as being real. Your assertion that the thorn does not, in fact, exist is all it takes to banish the thorn.

This is denial, not biblical faith. We don't have to evade the issue when we are sick or suffering. Pain is pain, no matter how much we may want it to disappear. It is wrong to gloss over suffering and call it something else. Yet that does not mean we have to be defeated by suffering, because God is more powerful than Satan.

2. God's Grace Takes Away the Sting

While Satan sends the thorns, God's grace overshadows the sting of the thorns. In the dark hour when Jesus died on the cross, Satan was celebrating. It appeared that he had triumphed, so Satan and his demonic hordes partied all night long. While it seemed just then that evil had gained the upper hand, the celebration was short-lived.

While Satan was celebrating, God was preparing for the Resurrection. God was intent on bringing good out of the greatest evil that could have happened, and that had been God's purpose all along.

Don't give up hope when Satan sends a thorn. Don't allow Satan's torments to make you doubt that God will bring good out of bad. Don't permit Satan to convince you that God doesn't love you enough to give you grace for every moment—because He *does* love you that much, and His grace *will* sustain you.

When Paul saw how God was using that painful thorn for His glory, Paul was able to rejoice in the midst of suffering. He stopped focusing on the thorn and began to focus on the sufficiency of God's grace. Seeing the hand of God at work, Paul lifted his eyes from the thorn and fixed his gaze on the throne of God.

The apostle asked God three times to remove the thorn, but God told him, "I will take away the sting of the thorn." Paul rejoiced that his prayers were answered. Not in the way or in the time he had wanted, but he knew God had answered. The Lord showed Paul the purpose of the thorn. Paul had received many visions and revelations from God, and the apostle understood that they could easily have sent him on the world's biggest ego trip. That's why the Lord told Paul, "I am using what Satan meant for evil to bring good. What Satan meant as torment, I will use to bless you and others."

Whatever thorns are causing you to suffer, God is using them to bless you. God will use the thorns for your own protection. You may be weary of the thorns, but be assured that God can take away the sting.

3. God's Grace Brings Roses out of Thorns

Notice that as Paul prayed about his thorn in the flesh, *he did not ask for grace*. Instead, he did what you and I would do, which is to plead with God: "Remove this thorn now, Lord. I can't take it anymore."

Paul did not ask for grace, but God gave him grace anyway. God provided the strength Paul needed to praise Him in spite of the thorn. Grace is the spiritual power to live triumphantly no matter what our circumstances. Grace is the spiritual ability to see the rose that is about to blossom in the midst of the briar patch.

We learn from Paul's example of a figurative thorn in the flesh, but we also remember that Christ once wore a literal crown of thorns. The Savior understands our suffering and identifies with our pain, and He liberally offers His grace to us whenever we need it. Without God's grace we could never rejoice in the midst of trials. We could never triumph over Satan's torment. God's grace is always more than sufficient to meet the need of the hour.

Without the torment of thorns, how could you experience the power of God's grace? Grace always shines the brightest against the darkness of our circumstances. That is why Paul was happy to boast about his weaknesses, so that Christ's power would rest upon him. If God's grace is not sufficient for you, then it may be that you are focusing so much on the thorn that you can't see the rose of God's grace developing in you.

Recently a series of thorns came my way all at once, while I was in the process of writing this book. I had traveled to Europe to tape a series of programs for our international broadcast ministry. Because of a security situation that arose while we were there, we were forced to drastically abbreviate our taping schedule, and I wound up having to record for thirteen straight hours in order to complete the series before we left the location.

Naturally, I was exhausted at the end of the marathon session. Not to mention that my wife and I were both suffering from a severe respiratory infection we acquired during our travels. Then, when I got back to the hotel, I received a message that my mother-in-law was critically ill. The next thirty-six hours produced a flurry of urgent phone calls, hurried packing, and mad dashes for airplanes as my wife and I made arrangements to fly to London and then on to Sydney. God graciously allowed both of us to make it there in time to be with Elizabeth's precious mother as she slipped from this world into the next.

In the middle of all of this, thousands of miles away, a dear friend of ours was diagnosed with lung cancer. Was the timing of these incidents just an unfortunate coincidence? I don't think so. I believe Satan manufactured these thorns in an attempt to derail the team responsible for getting this book into print, and I share these incidents so you will understand that the concepts I'm writing about are not just pious platitudes. These are the spiritual principles I live by.

Whenever life's thorns are stinging the most, it's time to pray, "Lord, help me take my eyes off the thorn and fix them on the throne of your grace." Once our concerns are left at the feet of our Lord, we must then trust with complete assurance that His grace is entirely sufficient. Apart from trusting in God's grace, there is no peace, no rest, no contentment.

Now let's examine another potential detour from God's grace: the snare of legalism.

Eight

THE LIE OF LEGALISM

Looking at the Practice That Blinds Us to God's Grace

The two teenage boys had to step into the street to get around a sidewalk display where several women were admiring finely woven cotton shawls with silver appliqué work. The local handicrafts were popular with visitors to the Upper Nile region, and when the boys watched a woman struggle to figure out the correct amount of currency to put into the shopkeeper's hand, their suspicions were confirmed.

"Crazy tourists," the older one mumbled.

"Yeah, they probably paid twice what those shawls were worth," the other boy said.

The friends picked their way through the streets, which were more crowded than usual because of the Feast of the Virgin. Every August, tourists braved the heat to visit the convent just outside the city of Assiut and the adjoining cave where the holy family—Joseph, Mary, and the infant Jesus—were supposed to have stayed when they sought refuge in Egypt.

"Your brother Samir would make a math problem out of the tourists paying too much for shawls. 'Tell me, Michael, if one shawl normally sells for six pounds and two shawls for ten pounds, then what is the percentage of savings—'"

"Hey, cut it out. I haven't worked a math problem all summer, and I don't want to think about it now." But Michael knew that his friend

Joseph had his older brother pegged. Samir was a prominent economist and had a head for numbers. Michael frequently asked for his help with homework. In return, Samir would extract a promise from him, which often involved running an errand.

If there was nothing more interesting to do, Michael would run the errand for his brother. But if some other adventure beckoned, he could easily forget the agreement he had made with Samir. In fact, just that morning Michael had decided to pursue adventure. And this time it required a lie. He told his mother that he was going to a friend's house, but he was really headed to the movies with Joseph. His parents would be furious if they found out. Going to movies was near the top of their list of prohibited activities for Christians.

When the boys reached the theater, Michael hesitated, looking around to make sure no one he knew was outside. He pretended to read the poster advertising the film, but his mind was recalling something his mother had said a few days earlier.

"You don't listen to what I say," she had told him.

"I'm listening," Michael had replied. He stood quietly, waiting for his mother to finish her lecture so he could go have fun with his friends.

"No, Michael. You hear my words, but you don't listen." Then she had laid her hand on his head. "Lord," she began praying, "if this boy is not going to be the one to serve You as I have believed all these years, then take him now."

Michael couldn't believe it. His own mother was asking God to take his life if he didn't straighten up.

"Are you going to stand there all day?" Joseph called out. "Let's get our tickets so we can get a good seat."

"Okay," Michael replied. But he didn't move.

Joseph's voice rose in frustration. "Look, do you want to go to the movies or not?"

"Sure," Michael said as he walked toward the ticket window. "It's just complicated for me."

"It's not complicated. You hand over your money, and they give you a ticket." Joseph plopped some coins onto the counter. "See?" Flashing a grin, he reached for the ticket and waved it at Michael.

Michael paid his admission and the boys entered the theater. Like most of the Christians in Egypt, Joseph attended a Coptic church, which didn't prohibit such activities as going to the movies. But Michael's family belonged to a small fundamentalist church—a fact he had often lamented due to its strict, legalistic rules.

"You know why this is tricky for me," Michael told his friend. "Somebody from my church might see me."

Joseph sighed. "Did it ever occur to you that if it's a sin for you to be here, then they're not supposed to be here either? They won't tell on you for fear you might tell on them—you have nothing to worry about."

"Well, when you put it that way…" Michael couldn't help smiling.

He'd been to the movies in Cairo before, but that was easier since Cairo was a huge city and no one knew him there. But in his hometown it seemed everybody knew everybody else. It was more difficult to be a rebel when someone was likely to discover your transgressions, but in a way, that made it more exciting.

The boys found good seats in the open-air theater, and Michael began to relax. When the first image appeared on the silver screen, he realized he had not caught the name of the film, so he asked Joseph.

"*Nahr Al Hob* with Faten Hamama and Omar El-Sharif. He's become famous worldwide since *Lawrence of Arabia* last year." Joseph was a movie buff, and he chattered happily about one of Egypt's most popular movie stars making the transition to English-speaking films.

Nahr Al Hob means "river of love." Michael leaned back and stretched his legs. The story was about a cruel man and his long-suffering wife, played by Faten Hamama, Egypt's leading actress, who falls in love with a young army officer, played by her real-life husband, Omar El-Sharif.

When a larger-than-life closeup of Sharif filled the screen, the woman next to Michael sighed dreamily. "He is so gorgeous," she whispered to her friend.

About halfway through the movie, Michael began to fidget. It was eerie, but the actor playing the woman's mean husband had a mannerism that reminded him of the pastor he often heard preach passionate sermons on sin. Michael blinked and looked at the screen again. He heard the actors speaking, yet it was the preacher's voice that filled his head.

Michael usually paid attention to sermons, since the pastor got so loud and animated that no one could ignore him. The cinema was one of the sins that particularly agitated this man. "What business do you have going to the devil's house?" the pastor often thundered. "What would happen if Jesus returned while you were staring at that sin-soaked screen? I'll tell you what would happen. You'd split hell wide open!"

Throughout the remainder of the movie, Michael couldn't quit thinking about Jesus coming back while he was sitting there and staring at the huge screen in "the devil's house." Now if he could just get home without his mother finding out where he'd been...

⟿

As you have probably surmised, I was the Egyptian teenager who couldn't enjoy watching movies because I had been so steeped in legalism. My father belonged to a church that believed you could fall in and out of grace, depending on your conduct. I was taught that if I went to the movies, smoked cigarettes, or played cards, I would lose my salvation. But that wasn't all. Making a purchase—even out of necessity—on the Lord's day meant I had fallen from grace.

The preacher at my dad's church often referred to the cinema as the devil's house. Keep in mind that these were all G-rated movies back then. Even as an adult, the few times that I dared to enter "the devil's house" to see even the most decent of movies, I was never able to enjoy the film and usually left before it ended.

Those who grow up in legalism continue to struggle with it for a long time, even after they become adults and are free to choose a more balanced view of the Christian life. I once heard Howard Hendricks, esteemed professor at Dallas Theological Seminary, comment on the grip of legalism. "I repudiated legalism intellectually and theologically in 1946," he said. "But in 1982 I am still wrestling with it emotionally."[1]

Legalism creeps into many Christian teachings, and it can blind us to God's grace. If we are on a journey to God's heart, finding contentment in his love and acceptance, legalism can detour us onto paths that lead far from the Lord. Legalism propagates the error of believing that salvation comes through God's grace plus our effort. It denies the truth of "grace alone, through faith alone," as the Protestant Reformers proclaimed the biblical doctrine of salvation.

LEGALISM VERSUS GRACE

Paul wrote his letter to the Christians in Galatia to combat the false doctrine of legalism—the faulty notion that God's grace is merely a beginning and that continuing the journey of the Christian life requires the force of our own effort, our own righteousness, or some other human achievement. It's the fallacy that salvation becomes effective through grace *plus* something else: believing a certain religious dogma; practicing a church ritual or sacrament; performing certain good deeds; avoiding certain behaviors or adopting peculiar outward appearances, such as hairstyles or requiring that women wear a head covering; and so forth.

Legalism is the elevation of man-made rules to the level of God's commands. When I was growing up, I believed that "thou shalt not smoke, thou shalt not drink, and thou shalt not play cards" were part of the biblical commandments.

In the church at Galatia, legalism involved a requirement that Christians—even Gentile believers—keep the Jewish ceremonial laws. Paul told the Galatians that trying to earn God's favor by strict adherence to the minutiae of the Mosaic Law was diametrically opposed to receiving God's favor through the gift of His grace. The two are mutually exclusive.

Grace is the teaching that God forgives us and sustains us and that God's grace will ultimately take us to glory. Legalism, on the other hand, imposes stringent rules and regulations. Some legalists insist that you eat certain foods or refrain from eating certain foods, that you observe certain holidays, or that you agree to stop celebrating certain occasions. Salvation can hinge on the clothes you wear, the music you listen to, or the way you wear your hair. Only if you faithfully adhere to the legalists' list of dos and don'ts can you be assured of salvation.

Scripture points out the lie of legalism. We are saved by grace alone, through faith alone, and even that faith is not our own; it is God's gift to us. We were dead in our sins, incapable of belief, until God breathed His faith into our lives.

A man was giving his testimony once in a legalistic church. As he spoke, he gave all the glory to God and never once claimed that he did anything to deserve God's grace. After he finished, the pastor said, "You told us about the grace of God in your life, but what about your part? You didn't say anything about that."

"Yes, I did," the man insisted. "For more than thirty years I ran away from God as fast as my sin could carry me. That was my part. But God took out after me and ran me down. That was His part!"

This man understood that there was nothing he could do that would qualify him to receive God's grace; it was a free gift, and he rejoiced in it.

FALLING FROM GRACE

Legalists frequently tell their followers that if they fail to adhere to the man-made requirements and prohibitions, they are in danger of losing their salvation. This is often referred to as falling from grace. But such use of this phrase creates confusion.

In his epistle to the Galatians, Paul explained the meaning of the phrase *fallen from grace.* Some people believe that a Christian can forfeit her salvation. But that teaching runs contrary to the words of Jesus in the gospel of John: "All that the Father gives me will come to me, and whoever comes to me I will never drive away. For I have come down from heaven not to do my will but to do the will of him who sent me. And this is the will of him who sent me, that I shall lose none of all that he has given me, but raise them up at the last day."[2]

It's tragic that many Christians lack joy, peace, and hope simply because they don't know if they will go to heaven. But God tells us that we *can* be assured of our salvation. We should be confident "that he who began a good work in you will carry it on to completion until the day of Christ Jesus."[3] God finishes what He starts, and His grace is "able to keep you from falling and to present you before his glorious presence without fault and with great joy."[4]

If Paul did not use the expression "fallen from grace" to mean that a Christian could lose his salvation, what did he mean? It's clear from the context that he was talking about legalism. Notice carefully what he wrote: "You who are trying to be justified by law have been alienated from Christ; you have fallen away from grace."[5] To sin and then to repent and ask for God's grace in forgiveness is not falling from grace. But to rely on your own ability to adhere to certain rules and rituals as the basis of your righteousness is a clear step away from God's grace. It's an indication that you are relying on your own discipline in following rules. This is a denial of God and his gift of grace. Since choosing legalism is to abandon grace as the basis of our relationship with God, then you have turned away, or fallen away, from belief in the all-sufficient work of Christ in salvation.

THE ORIGIN OF LEGALISM

The legalists of Jesus' day were the Pharisees. On more than one occasion Jesus lambasted them, calling them hypocrites, snakes, fools, and blind guides. He was angry because the Pharisees loaded the people with rules that weren't found in Scripture.

When Paul preached the gospel in Asia Minor, many people received salvation by grace and the church was established. But not long after that, the churches in the area, especially the congregation at Galatia, fell prey to the teaching of the Judaizers. These were Jewish believers—most likely from the sect of the Pharisees—who insisted that only those who kept the Jewish law could be saved. Like their modern-day successors, these Judaizers were deceptive. First, they undermined Paul's credibility, then they undermined the gospel he preached.

Many years ago I was preaching on the biblical instruction regarding the spiritual headship of the husband in the home. A handful of folks who didn't like what I was preaching went around undermining my credibility in order to undermine the biblical truth I was teaching. They said things like, "Oh, he's from the Middle East and just doesn't understand Western culture." They also tried to discredit what the Bible says about the husband's spiritual authority, a principle the Bible teaches from Genesis to Revelation. I'm happy to say those people are no longer in our congregation. They illustrate the enemy's tactics against the truth. First, undermine the preacher of the truth, then attack the truth itself.

In the epistle to the Galatians, Paul became more indignant than ever. He used strong language to disabuse his readers of the notion that keeping the Law could save them. "You foolish Galatians! Who has bewitched you?" he asked. "After beginning with the Spirit, are you now trying to attain your goal by human effort?"[6]

Paul was adamant on this point because the teaching that salvation is through grace plus something else repudiates the gospel of Jesus Christ. When you add any other requirement to the completed work of Christ on the cross, you deny the truth of salvation and empty the Cross of its power. That is why Paul was so emphatic in Galatians 5, saying that if a person is trying to be saved by works, she has fallen from grace into legalism and therefore cannot be saved, since no one can be saved by legalism.

Many years ago my wife and I were members of a legalistic, ritualistic mainline denomination. The leaders did not believe in the authority of Scripture or the divinity of Christ. They did not believe that Jesus is the only way to salvation. But whenever I strayed from the tradition governing the church's rituals, they would find fault with me, and I'd get a letter in the mail or a phone call from the leadership. They must have had spies in my congregation. It is such a sad thing that two thousand years after the New Testament so clearly spelled out that salvation is through grace alone, some people are still preaching salvation through the keeping of legalistic rituals.

LEGALISM IS MAN'S WAY, NOT GOD'S WAY

Years ago a missionary in Africa was trying to explain the Christian life to a tribal chief. After many hours of listening to the missionary, the aged chief said, "I don't understand. You told me that I must not take my neighbor's wife or his oxen. You said I must not dance the war dance or ambush my enemy and kill him."

"That's right," the missionary responded.

"But I can't do any of those things anymore," the worn-out warrior said. "I'm too old for that. Being too old and being a Christian must be the same thing."

By focusing on dos and don'ts—even though his list outlined good moral conduct—the missionary had failed to convey the grace of God. The missionary had presented *his* version of salvation, not the scriptural truth of salvation. By reading Scripture we can see the difference between man's way and God's way. Legalism is man's way, not God's.

Beginning in the fourth century, the monastic movement began to influence Christianity, spreading the doctrine of asceticism, the practice of strict self-denial as a spiritual discipline. We read of monks who lived on a diet of bread, salt, and water. They often slept on the bare ground or went without sleep altogether. Some wore only a loincloth or a shirt made of rough animal hair. Still others let their hair grow long and wore it as their only clothing.

The monks went to these lengths as an effort to do special things to please God, to earn God's favor through their disciplined lifestyle. Like legalism, asceticism is man's way, not God's way.

God's grace is undeserved. There is nothing we can do to earn it. However, many people have gone to the other extreme of interpreting God's grace as a license to sin. But that is equally erroneous.

THE OPPOSITE ERROR OF LEGALISM

If we have been saved by the free gift of grace, as Scripture teaches, there are always those who ask: "Can't we just go on and break every commandment without suffering any consequences? If we've received salvation, we'll still go to heaven, won't we?"

Asking this question demonstrates that a person has not had a direct encounter with God's grace. If you believe you have the right to ignore God's commandments, you are not saved. This is license, the opposite of legalism. The technical name for this heresy is antinomianism, which comes from two Greek words that literally mean "against the law" *(anti + nomos)*. In the first century adherents of this belief were sometimes called "libertines," and in Galatians the apostle Paul warned them not to use the liberty of God's grace as a license to sin. "Do not use your freedom to indulge the sinful nature," Paul wrote. "Rather, serve one another in love. The entire law is summed up in a single command: 'Love your neighbor as yourself.'"[7]

Although we are not saved by keeping the Law, the Bible tells us that those who have been saved by grace *do* keep God's commandments. They keep not only the letter of the Law but the spirit of the Law as well. A person who has experienced God's grace does not just obey the commandment not to covet his neighbor's possessions; he follows Christ in loving his neighbor sacrificially.[8] But Christians are not left to do this alone. The Holy Spirit empowers us to do what is not humanly possible: to live in obedience to God.

God's grace provides the desire and gives us the power to obey Him. The Holy Spirit helps us to be all God intended us to be, which is to be free.

THE FREEDOM OF GOD'S GRACE

Freedom is a precious word. In the natural realm, freedom does not come without cost. We are privileged to live in a free country, but only because our forefathers made the ultimate sacrifice to secure America's freedom. As the Declaration of Independence says, they pledged their lives, their fortunes, and their sacred honors to birth this nation. Already in the new millennium, young men and women from America, Great Britain, Australia, and other countries have laid down their lives to bring freedom to the Iraqi people. Political freedom is costly.

Spiritual freedom is also costly, but it was God Himself who paid the price. Jesus took all our sins upon Himself and gave His life on a cruel cross so that you and I might be free. He purchased our salvation and then turned around and freely gave it to us.

God is not stingy with His grace. Paul told the Ephesians that God has "freely given us" His "glorious grace."[9] In fact, He "lavished" this grace on us, Paul said.[10] God lavished the riches of His grace on us so that we would be free to serve. Free to love. Free to sacrifice. Free to obey. "It is for freedom that Christ has set us free," Paul wrote the Galatians. "Stand firm, then, and do not let yourselves be burdened again by a yoke of slavery."[11]

Some people think it's difficult to adhere to the demands of legalism. Quite the contrary. Legalism is easy. It is relatively easy not to murder, but it is hard to obey with the heart by reaching out to love someone who despises you. It is relatively easy not to commit adultery, but it is hard to keep loving your spouse more than you love yourself. It is relatively easy to pay taxes, which carry a legal penalty if you fail to file a tax return. But it is much harder to give sacrificially to the work of God, denying yourself a portion of your income to advance the work of the kingdom.

To experience true freedom in Christ is to be in constant openness to the Holy Spirit's guidance, even if I don't like where He leads me. Living in the Spirit makes me more conscious of what I have left undone, rather than feeling proud of what I have accomplished.

I've heard it said that the ultimate effect of legalism is to lower our view of God. I could not agree more. Grace, however, elevates our view of God to the heights of adoration. I have preached on several continents, written books, launched worldwide radio and television programs, and built churches. I'm glad to have done all that, yet none of what I have done is impressive. What overwhelms me is not how much I have accomplished but how much God's grace has done for me. He has lavished upon me His unmerited favor when I am in no way deserving of it.

Legalism kills our sense of wonder and gratitude. If we're not careful, we'll take the detour of legalism and lose the path that leads to God's heart. Relying on God and His grace brings peace and quiets our restlessness. Relying on self and our ability to fulfill rules and regulations robs our spirit and creates anxiety that steals our peace. The path to God is the path of grace, which leads to peace and contentment.

Legalism will set us back on a path of wandering away from God rather than on the path of trust in His grace. Don't take the detour. Don't trade the peace of returning to God for the bondage of legalism.

Nine

THE PITFALL OF PRIDE

Why Prayer Is Such a Struggle

Queen Esther paced the floor, the soles of her jeweled sandals clicking out a rhythm on the smooth marble. She desperately wanted to talk to her cousin Mordecai, a high-ranking official in the king's court, but he couldn't enter the palace while he was dressed in mourning. Yesterday she had sent new garments to Mordecai, begging him through her servant to come and see her. But he had refused to take off his sackcloth. Instead, he remained outside the palace gate, wailing bitterly.

Something terrible must have happened or Mordecai would never have refused her request. He was like a father to her, having raised her after she was orphaned. When they had been among the captives sent into exile after King Nebuchadnezzar conquered Israel, Mordecai had protected Esther throughout the long trek to Persia. She had been known as Hadassah then, and she had lived with her cousin in the royal city of Susa—until she had been chosen for the king's harem and then elevated to queen.

Suddenly Esther stopped pacing and summoned one of her maids. "Get Hathach for me."

When the eunuch arrived, he bowed respectfully. "What is your wish, Majesty?"

"Go to my cousin Mordecai," she instructed the servant. "He will be in the city square, just outside the palace gates. Find out why he is mourning. Implore him to send an answer."

Esther resumed her pacing. The thought of something happening to Mordecai terrified her. Wearily, she dropped onto a reclining sofa.

Before long, Hathach returned with a message. "He told me everything that has happened," the eunuch reported. "He also gave me a copy of this edict and asked me to explain it to you. Shall I read it?"

Esther nodded, and in a somber tone Hathach read the order from the king to annihilate all the Jews—young and old, women and children—on a single day, the thirteenth of Adar.

How could Xerxes have done this? Why would he want to destroy her people? Would he really let her be killed?

Slowly it dawned on Esther that the king did not know she was Jewish. When she had been taken into the palace, Esther had obeyed Mordecai's instructions not to mention her family background. So the king could not have known that he was signing her death warrant with his edict. One of the king's advisors had probably deceived him into issuing the decree.

"Who convinced the king to sign this edict?" the queen asked her servant.

"Mordecai said it was Haman. He promised to pay ten thousand talents of silver into the royal treasury for the men who carry out the order. Mordecai said something else, Majesty. He urges you to go before the king's throne and beg for mercy for your people."

"But that's impossible," she said. "Anyone who approaches the king in the inner court without being summoned will be put to death. The only exception is for the king to extend his scepter and spare the petitioner's life."

"As you have said, Majesty."

Esther rose from the couch. "Take another message to Mordecai. Tell him that I cannot do what he asks. It has been some thirty days since the king has sent for me." Now she wondered if the king had discovered she was a Jew. Perhaps that was why he had not summoned her.

Hathach left and an hour later returned with a letter from Mordecai to the queen. Esther unrolled the parchment and read:

> Do not think that because you are in the king's house you alone of all the Jews will escape. For if you remain silent at this time, relief and deliverance for the Jews will arise from another place, but you and your father's family will perish. And who knows but that you have come to royal position for such a time as this?[1]

Esther dismissed the servant and thought about Mordecai's letter. If she went before the king uninvited and he did not receive her, she would be put to death. On the other hand, if she did not attempt to ask the king to amend the decree, then she and all of her people would perish.

Finally, Esther picked up a quill and wrote her reply: "Gather all the Jews in Susa and fast for me. Do not eat or drink for three days, night or day. My maids and I will also fast. After three days, I will go before the king, even though it is against the law."

She paused briefly, then completed the note: "And if I perish, I perish."[2]

After three days of fasting, Esther prepared to go before the king. Her attendants bathed her and rubbed her skin with oils and fragrance. She dressed in royal robes of purple and blue spun with threads of gold and put bangles on her arms and in her ears—ornaments the king had given her personally.

With a knot in her stomach, Esther crossed the palace's inner court and entered the king's hall. Xerxes was seated on his throne, facing the entrance. She moved forward until he noticed her, all the while not knowing if she was about to face a death sentence.

Evidently the king was pleased to see her, and he called her forward. Relief buoyed Esther as she saw him extend the scepter.

"What is it, my queen?" Xerxes asked. "What is your request? Even if it is for half my kingdom, I will give it to you."

Esther's heart was pounding, and she was aware that many eyes were on her. Instinctively, she held back, deciding not to present her petition in open court.

"If it pleases the king," she said, "let the king, together with Haman, come today to a banquet I have prepared for him."

She would ask Xerxes to spare her life and save her people, but she would do it privately. And she would make sure the king knew the diabolical nature of Haman's plot.

" 'Bring Haman at once,' the king said, 'so that we may do what Esther asks.' "[3]

FOR BELIEVERS ONLY

As we see in the story of Queen Esther, following God can move us from a place of safety into an area of danger. In Esther's case, being obedient to God could easily have cost the queen her life. Yet with the support of many others who were followers of God, she took a courageous stand for what was right. Esther took a major risk, and untold lives were spared.

When we struggle in life, it's not always because we are rejecting God's way in order to fulfill our own desires. Wanting to follow God can give rise to an incredible inner struggle. Few of us are called to take a courageous, highly visible stand such as that of Queen Esther. Yet we are often called to stand up for what is right, to oppose injustice, to obey God in word and deed even when that puts us in a place of risk.

In previous chapters we saw that restlessness is not always a sign of disobedience. The stories of Abraham, Joseph, Ruth, and others show that obeying God can cause tremendous disruption. Our discontent can come from God as a prompting that He wants us to make a change, to shift direction, or to take a stand. But if we start feeling that we deserve better or that God is somehow shortchanging us and decide to shift directions in an effort to find contentment, we are probably following our own sinful nature.

Human pride resides within all of us, since we all have inherited a sin nature. Not only is pride a powerful force, it is also deceptive. We can talk ourselves into believing that our choices are motivated by a desire to do good when, in fact, we are motivated by a desire to do what's best for ourselves. Setting aside our own agenda starts with accepting God's invitation to come boldly before His throne of grace. With such an invitation extended to us, how can we possibly neglect the pursuit of prayer? Why would we refuse to enter into God's chamber, the King's throne room, when He issues such an open invitation? Part of the problem is that life can become too comfortable.

THE CHALLENGE OF PRAYER

Ask the average Christian how long she spends in personal prayer time when everything is going well. You'll probably be met with a sheepish look and a good deal of hemming and hawing. Some Christians are consistent in prayer, but most are crisis prayer warriors.

There are several reasons for this. For one thing, the enemy of our souls knows that prayer is the source of our strength. Therefore, Satan does all that is within his power to cut our supply lines. If the enemy can keep us from praying, he can block God's outpouring of blessing on our lives.

The second enemy of prayer is pride. Pride tells us that we can solve any problem, accomplish anything we set our mind to. We let ourselves believe that everything we need can be achieved through human effort if we just invest enough time and enough energy. That sounds logical, but it's a lie. It's no wonder we get into such desperate spiritual trouble.

The third and perhaps most significant enemy of prayer is that we don't comprehend the awesome privilege of praying. We simply do not understand the marvelous provisions God has made possible for us in prayer, nor do we understand His eagerness to answer our prayers. We fail to appreciate the power of connectedness with the Almighty that comes through prayer.

In a time of grave crisis, Queen Esther approached the king's throne with fear and trepidation. It was against the law to come before the king without an invitation. Had the king not extended the royal scepter, signifying his willingness to grant her an audience, she could have been put to death. But the king was pleased to see her, even though she appeared unannounced and uninvited.

If a human king could extend grace to an uninvited visitor, how much more is God willing to extend grace to us when we approach Him in prayer? After all, we have an explicit and unlimited invitation to come before God's throne and to beseech Him for whatever we need.

To begin to comprehend the power of the grace of God in prayer, let's look at the invitation God has extended.

> Therefore, since we have a great high priest who has gone through the heavens, Jesus the Son of God, let us hold firmly to the faith we profess. For we do not have a high priest who is unable to sympathize with our weaknesses, but we have one who has been tempted in every way, just as we are—yet was without sin. Let us then approach the throne of grace with confidence, so that we may receive mercy and find grace to help us in our time of need.[4]

This is an open-ended invitation to all who are followers of the Lord Jesus Christ. We are invited to experience the awesomeness of the power of the grace of God in prayer. We need not approach God in fear, worrying whether He will receive us or whether we can find the proper words to utter. When we have received Christ as our Savior, we are invited to enter the royal throne room. We have a right to be there, and it is our privilege to pour our hearts out to God in prayer.

A CONVERTED THRONE

Few of us today have a clear concept of the throne of God. In the West, especially, we have only a vague notion of what a throne looks like, much less its function. Tourists to Buckingham Palace may see the royal throne room, where the queen of England sits on a massive red-and-gold-draped dais for the rare state occasion. But the throne room of Buckingham Palace has been reduced to mere ceremonial usage; the real power in England lies elsewhere.

When we speak of God's throne, of course, we are using a figure of speech to describe the sovereignty of God. Our heavenly Father is spiritual in nature, not physical or corporeal, so of course He does not literally sit on a throne. Yet the most common image we have of God is of a foreboding, white-haired man dispensing judgment while sitting on an opulent golden throne. No wonder most people cower at the thought of approaching God in prayer. I wouldn't want to talk to that kind of deity either!

But that is not a proper image of God or of His throne. It's true that the throne is the seat of God's power and judgment. However, the New Testament shows us that the throne of judgment has been converted into the throne of grace for those who belong to Christ.

CONVERTING A THRONE OF JUDGMENT

Menelik II ruled Ethiopia from 1889 to 1913. When he heard about a new device used in the West to punish criminals, the emperor ordered one for his country. But when the new device—an electric chair—arrived, it was unusable; Ethiopia had no source of electricity. Spurred by his purchase, Menelik set about to bring electricity to his country. In the meantime, the electric chair did not go to waste. The emperor had it converted into a throne.

That highly unusual throne must have been quite a sight. It was certainly a creative endeavor, turning an instrument of torture and death into a throne for the king. But the conversion of God's seat of judgment to a throne of grace was no accident. It was not an attempt to rectify a mistake; rather, this conversion was planned before the world began.

Scripture describes the throne of God as a seat of judgment, a throne of condemnation for some. The book of Revelation says: "Then I saw a great white throne and him who was seated on it.... And I saw the dead, great and small, standing before the throne, and books were opened. Another book was opened, which is the book of life. The dead were judged according to what they had done as recorded in the books."[5]

These books contain documentation of the evidence brought against those who are to be judged. Those whose names are written in "the book of life"—those who have trusted Jesus as their Savior—are not subject to this judgment. But the unredeemed—the ones who have rejected Jesus Christ—will be judged according to their deeds as recorded in the other books. "If anyone's name was not found written in the book of life, he was thrown into the lake of fire."[6]

The coming judgment is a dreadful scene that unbelievers should, rightfully, fear. But Hebrews 4:16 tells us that the throne of judgment, for those who love the Lord Jesus, has become the throne of grace. To those who trust in Christ, the throne of condemnation has become the throne of mercy.

The throne of grace represents the seat of God's unmerited favor and kindness toward us. The throne signifies His unlimited forgiveness and the undeserved blessings and untold power and strength He extends to us.

FROM JUDGMENT TO GRACE

Esther approached a human king hoping for grace but knowing that the judgment of death could await her instead. We approach the throne of the King of the universe knowing that He invites us to approach and promises grace to us, not judgment. The throne of judgment has become a throne of grace in three ways, and each one draws us to God.

1. God Loves to Give His Children Gifts When They Ask Him

Here is how Jesus described God's willingness to extend grace and mercy to us: "Which of you, if his son asks for bread, will give him a stone? Or if he asks for a fish, will give him a snake? If you, then, though you are evil, know how to give good gifts to your children, how much more will your Father in heaven give good gifts to those who ask him!"[7]

Why should we put off coming to God in prayer until we are absolutely desperate? It makes no sense! Not only do we have an unlimited invitation into God's throne room, we have assurance that our heavenly Father delights in giving us what we need. He is not stingy with His blessings, nor does He give begrudgingly. God is more than ready to answer our prayers; all we have to do is accept His invitation to come before His throne in prayer.

2. Jesus, Our High Priest, Sits on the Right Hand of the Throne

Our High Priest understands us and identifies with us in our weaknesses. As our great High Priest, Jesus is waiting for us to come before the throne of grace not for condemnation but for blessing. He wants us to come to the throne to receive power over temptation because He understands temptation and has triumphed over it. He wants to give us victory over the trials of life. Remember the life-changing truth of Hebrews 4:15: "For we do not have a high priest who is unable to sympathize with our weaknesses, but we have one who has been tempted in every way, just as we are—yet was without sin."

All we have to do is ask for His help; it's that simple. We try to make prayer complicated when it should be as natural as talking to someone we love.

3. The Holy Spirit Assists Us in Prayer

Because God's throne is a throne of grace, all our faults and flawed attempts to phrase our prayers "just so" will not hinder the success of our petitions to God. His heavenly throne room does not entertain the pomp or protocols of earthly kingdoms. If we cannot find words to adequately state our needs to God, the Holy Spirit will interpret them for us.

Have you ever watched a young child who was first learning to talk? Sometimes you knew the little one had something to say, but he struggled so hard to verbalize it. After a while you would help out by suggesting a word or helping him sound out the syllables, and his little face would light up when he knew he had communicated what was on his heart.

In the same way, the Holy Spirit assists us in prayer when we can't find the right words to express our heart's desire. "We do not know what we ought to pray for," Paul wrote to the Romans, "but the Spirit himself intercedes for us with groans that words cannot express."[8]

Scripture also describes the Holy Spirit as our Counselor and Comforter. The gospel of John records this promise of Jesus: "And I will ask the Father, and he will give you another Counselor to be with you forever—

the Spirit of truth."[9] This promise refers to the indwelling presence of the Holy Spirit in the believer's life.

The King James Version translates the Greek word used in this verse as *Comforter;* the New International Version uses *Counselor.* Both are accurate translations of the term *parakletos,* which in ancient times referred to a friend who appeared on someone's behalf or a person who served as a mediator or advisor.

When we think of the Holy Spirit as our Comforter, we often have in mind the idea of consolation, and it is true that solace for our grief is a spiritual blessing bestowed by God.[10] But the primary meaning of our English word *comfort* is not consolation but more closely related to the Latin *confortare,* which means "to strengthen greatly." As our Comforter, the Holy Spirit strengthens us so that we may endure our troubles; then we can strengthen others with the same strength we have received. How do we receive this strength? We find it when we come to the throne of God, and we come "with confidence, so that we may receive mercy and find grace to help us in our time of need."[11]

Notice the role of our triune God—Father, Son, and Holy Spirit—in converting the throne of judgment into the throne of grace. Each member of the Godhead has a part in hearing and answering our prayers. God the Father wants to give His children good gifts. As our High Priest, God the Son understands our suffering and our weaknesses, and He opens the door for us to receive the abundance of His awesome grace. And God the Holy Spirit strengthens and comforts us during all our troubles as we turn to Him in prayer.

THE MERCY SEAT

The Old Testament teachings associated with the mercy seat open our eyes to the awesomeness of the grace of God. The Old Testament foreshadows the New Testament, and the throne of grace that we see in Hebrews has its origin in the ancient ark of the covenant, the sole piece of furniture kept in the Most Holy Place of the temple. The ark was a wooden box about three feet long and eighteen inches deep. It was used to hold the stone tablets of the Law of Moses. The lid of the ark was pure gold, and on top of the lid were two golden figures of cherubim facing each other.

The ark was of paramount importance in Israel's worship, for God was symbolically present between the cherubim. As God looked down on His people from between the outstretched wings of the cherubim, He would see the Law that He had given to Moses—a set of commandments that every person has broken. That is why the lid of the ark functioned as the judgment seat of God; the people stood convicted by their inability to keep the Law perfectly.

Here's the fascinating point: The lid of the ark was known not only as the judgment seat of God. For one day each year, it was also called the mercy seat. On the Day of Atonement, after the high priest had sacrificed an animal for his own sins and the sins of the people, he brought the blood of the slain animal into the Most Holy Place and sprinkled it on the mercy seat. At the moment the high priest sprinkled the blood on the lid of the ark, the ark was no longer a picture of judgment. Instead, it became a symbol of grace and mercy, signifying that God would forgive the sins of His people.

But that happened only once a year! Only on that one day did the throne of judgment become the throne of grace, because of the blood of an innocent sacrifice that was slain for the sins of the people, and God accepted the sacrifice as atonement for their sins.

The New Testament, however, tells us that God the Son shed His own blood as the perfect and complete sacrifice for our sins. Speaking of Jesus as our High Priest, the book of Hebrews says: "Day after day every priest stands and performs his religious duties; again and again he offers the same sacrifices, which can never take away sins. But when this priest [Jesus Christ] had offered for all time one sacrifice for sins, he sat down at the right hand of God."[12] Unlike the other high priests, Jesus did not have to atone for His own sin because He had none. By shedding His own blood for us, He *permanently* transformed the throne of judgment into the throne of grace for all who put their trust in Him. The throne of judgment was changed forever. It will always be the throne of grace for all believers.

HOW TO APPROACH GOD'S THRONE

The writer of Hebrews invites all who have put their trust in Jesus Christ to draw near to the throne of God with confidence. If you try to come on your own merits, you cannot have confidence that your prayers will be heard. If you try to come based on how good you are, you will be barred access. But if you come trusting only in what Jesus has done for you, if you come with confidence because of the shedding of Christ's blood for you, then you will find grace in times of need.

Are you distraught and fearful, confused and anxious? There is comfort, wisdom, and discernment for you at the throne. Are you discouraged and about to give up? There is encouragement for you at the throne. Are you weak and defeated? There is victory for you at the throne of grace.

In times of difficulty, we recognize our need for prayer. But we often feel our prayers are falling on deaf ears. We must approach God's throne on the basis of Christ's shed blood, and we must ask the King for help. "You do not have, because you do not ask God," James wrote. "When you ask, you do not receive, because you ask with wrong motives, that you may spend what you get on your pleasures."[13]

TAKING GOD AT HIS WORD

An ancient legend tells of a monarch who hired workers to make tapestries and garments for the royal household. Among the workers was a young boy who was especially skilled at weaving. The king provided the workers with large spools of colorful silk and patterns for intricate designs. He also instructed them to ask him for help as soon as any problem arose.

The hardworking young boy made steady progress while the others experienced distress over their many failures. One day the other tapestry makers gathered around the youngster and asked, "Why are you so successful while we are always having trouble? Either our thread becomes tangled or our weaving varies from the pattern—there is always something wrong."

The lad thought for a minute and said, "Don't you remember that the king told us to go to him whenever we needed help?"

"Well, yes," they said to the boy. "We finally asked for his assistance, but by then the silk had become so snarled that it took us days to unravel our mistakes."

"Did you notice how often I called for him?" the boy asked.

"Well, yes," the other weavers protested, "and we thought you were arrogant to keep on disturbing him."

"Well, I took him at his word, and he was always happy to help me."

The young boy frequently approached the king for help. If an earthly king was happy to be taken at his word, how much more readily will the King of the universe respond to such trust? He invites us to come in. Why do we hesitate?

When we begin to understand the awesome grace and mercy of God, we will not hesitate to run to the throne of grace. It will become a regular habit. God has promised that we will find help in our time of need when we approach His throne with confidence. And when we make prayer the pattern of our lives, we will learn to extend the comfort and strength we find to others who are struggling and stumbling through difficult times.

> Therefore, brothers, since we have confidence to enter the Most
> Holy Place by the blood of Jesus…let us draw near to God with a
> sincere heart in full assurance of faith, having our hearts sprinkled
> to cleanse us from a guilty conscience and having our bodies
> washed with pure water. Let us hold unswervingly to the hope we
> profess, for he who promised is faithful. And let us consider how
> we may spur one another on toward love and good deeds.[14]

Christ has opened the way for us to bring our journey full circle, from the intimate communion of the Garden of Eden, through the wilderness of sin, to complete, open access to God's throne in prayer. We can draw near with confidence, not in shame or fear. And once we discover the peace and power of God's grace, we can help guide other spiritual sojourners who have not yet found that the destination they truly long for is the heart of God's grace.

Ten

CHEATING OURSELVES
OUT OF BLESSING

How Generosity Delivers Contentment

The rabbi from Nazareth was teaching again, and Miryam joined the group gathered in Solomon's Porch to listen. Her feet ached after standing throughout the temple sacrifices, but she was determined to stay until she had a chance to make her offering. She could have done so already, but she didn't want to place her meager gift into the treasury until the crowds had thinned. As a widow, she seldom had the requisite two *lepta* for the minimum offering, and it was not lawful to give only one of the small copper coins. But today she would make her offering, and that would be an occasion for rejoicing and giving thanks to God.

Listening to the rabbi while she waited seemed a good way to pass the time. She had heard this Jesus of Nazareth a few times before, and she enjoyed hearing what he had to say. Miryam took a position beside one of the soaring marble pillars that lined the colonnade around the Court of the Gentiles. Leaning against the pillar eased some of the burden on her tired feet.

The elderly woman studied the crowd while the rabbi from Galilee spoke. She had observed some of his followers before, and they were a strange sort with their country accents and unpolished ways. Yet they were obviously devoted to God and their rabbi, and they had been friendly to her. The one named Levi—a former tax collector, she had learned—had helped her climb the stairs to the gate one day, and he had kindly addressed her as "mother."

As Miryam watched the rabbi, she noticed that some teachers of the Law were asking him pointed questions. He answered patiently but firmly. Then one of the questioners stepped forward and said, "Teacher, we know you are a man of integrity, and you teach the way of God in accordance with the truth."

Miryam scoffed at the man's blatant insincerity. His demeanor showed that he was as haughty and self-important as his fellow scholars. He probably considered Jesus a threat to his respected status as a teacher of the Law.

"Tell us," the man continued, "is it right to pay taxes to Caesar or not?"

A murmur of approval arose from the other teachers, and Jesus gazed intently at the man. "Why are you trying to trap me?" the rabbi asked.

When the man offered no reply, Jesus said, "Bring me a denarius and let me look at it."

Someone handed the rabbi a coin, and he inspected it, turning it over in his hand. Then Jesus held the denarius up in front of the crowd. "Whose portrait is this?" he asked. "And whose inscription?"

"Caesar's," several people replied.

Jesus handed the coin back to its owner and turned toward the original questioner. "Give to Caesar what is Caesar's and to God what is God's."[1]

The pompous man turned and left, and a number of his colleagues trailed after him. When they had departed, Jesus said, "Watch out for the teachers of the Law. They like to walk around in flowing robes to be greeted in the marketplaces. They vie to have the most important seats in the synagogues and the places of honor at banquets. They make lengthy prayers for show, and they prey on widows."[2]

A lump rose in Miryam's throat. One of the teachers of the Law had paid repeated visits to her house, pressing her to make financial donations and trying to make her feel guilty for her supposed lack of generosity. She would love to be able to give more to the Lord, but with no husband and no son to support her, Miryam was a pauper. The man's visits always left her troubled and resentful.

She looked at Jesus and her eyes met his. "Such men will be punished most severely," the rabbi said solemnly, and Miryam could have sworn he knew exactly what she was thinking.

The group around Jesus began to dwindle, and the rabbi and his disciples made their way to the long flight of stairs leading from the porch to the gate of the city. The only people left were those making personal sacrifices and those, like Miryam, who had not yet deposited their offerings. She would not have minded if Jesus saw her make her offering, but she did not want to be observed by the teachers or the Pharisees. She slowly walked toward the Court of the Women and went inside.

From his vantage point on the stairway, Levi noticed the elderly woman entering the court below. The disciples had arranged themselves on the steps around Jesus—the only place sitting was permitted at the temple—so he could continue teaching in a more comfortable setting.

Levi could see into the large inner court, an area that could accommodate up to fifteen thousand worshipers. Thirteen trumpet-shaped receptacles, each with a wide mouth and narrowed bottom, were spaced out around the colonnade inside the Court of the Women. Each trumpet bore an inscribed number to indicate the type of offering to be placed inside, so it was possible to know what kind of contribution a worshiper made just by noting which trumpet was used. Two trumpets were designated for the annual half-shekel temple tribute; one was for women to pay the equivalent price for a turtledove offering; others were designed for contributions to purchase wood and incense for the temple; and still others were for sin offerings and voluntary offerings.

Before resuming his teaching, Jesus paused to note the worshipers as they made their offerings. Several rich people threw in large amounts of money, but Miryam approached one of the trumpets and deposited only two coins, slowly dropping in one after the other.

"I tell you the truth," Jesus said. "This poor widow has put more into the treasury than all the others. They all gave out of their wealth, but out of her poverty she put in everything—all she had to live on."[3]

⤳

Jesus commended the widow's generosity because He could see her heart. She gave out of her poverty, and she gave sacrificially. Her meager gift meant more to her and to the Lord because it was given out of scarcity.

We read about poverty in the newspaper, and some of us might drive through low-income neighborhoods as we commute to work or run errands. But most Americans are comfortably removed from the dire circumstances this woman faced. We don't have to choose between buying food or giving a gift to God. We can donate a portion of our income and still have plenty to live on. But even though most of us enjoy material comfort, most people fail to give generously. The level of comfort we experience can work against a healthy restlessness that drives us to give back to God a portion of what He has given to us.

Miryam, the name we've given to the devout widow whose story is told in the gospel of Luke, experienced some of that internal restlessness as she waited to give her gift at the temple. For one, she regretted that she was not able to give more. But as a widow, she barely had enough money to cover basic, survival-level needs. And to avoid having more shame heaped upon her, she waited until others dispersed before giving her small offering. But Jesus was still there, and He knew the woman's generosity.

The unease she felt internally was born of her desire to give even more to support the service of God's temple.

THE CURSE OF AFFLUENCE

To those who struggle for survival like the widow in this story, even a little seems like a lot when you are wondering how you'll be able to feed your family. In contrast, having more than we need—as is the case for most Americans—often brings with it a false sense that we can take credit for our material well-being. We forget to give thanks because we're too comfortable—we don't feel the pangs of hunger or the distress of being homeless. Affluence can quiet the healthy restlessness that draws us to rely on God's provision. If we keep accepting the gracious gifts of our heavenly Father—taking and taking without giving back and expressing heartfelt gratitude—before long we'll be spoiled brats, spiritually speaking.

In addition to verbally expressing our thanks to God, one of the best ways we can demonstrate our gratitude for His blessings and grace is through our giving. Giving is a key spiritual principle. Even psychologists and social scientists acknowledge this fact. The famous psychiatrist Karl Menninger once said, "Money giving is a very good criterion...of a person's mental health. Generous people are rarely mentally ill people."[4]

That observation flies in the face of the materialistic mentality that stresses acquisition, an attitude neatly summed up by the bumper sticker that says, "The one who dies with the most toys wins." Most people recognize that statement as patently false yet continue to live as if it were true. Life, however, is not a competition to accumulate possessions, and as Dr. Menninger pointed out, good mental health necessitates taking some of the money you spend on needless things and giving it away.

If holding onto your sanity is not enough motivation to loosen your death grip on your wallet, perhaps the words of Jesus will convince you. In the 2000 presidential election debates, Democratic nominee Al Gore misquoted Jesus' words, as most people do. Vice President Gore said, "Where your heart is, there is your treasure."[5] But Jesus actually said, "Where your money is, there you will find your heart."[6]

Note that He did not say, "Where your sermons are, you'll find your heart." Or "Where your high-profile ministry is, you'll find your heart." Jesus did not single out preaching or teaching or any other spiritual activity. Instead, He made it clear that how you spend your money demonstrates where your heart is. Many Christians need a spiritual heart transplant because their giving records show that their heart is in the wrong place.

Let me give you a humorous illustration of a typical tight-fisted Christian. A small-town pastor wanted to challenge an outspoken farmer in his congregation. When he visited the farm, the preacher asked the man, "Do you love Jesus enough to give Him your tithe?"

The farmer thrust out his chest and said, "I love Jesus so much that I wouldn't just give Him 10 percent. I'd give Him half of everything I own."

The pastor looked surprised. "You mean if you had a hundred horses you'd give Him fifty?"

"Yes, preacher, I would."

"Or if you had a hundred cows you'd give Him fifty?"

"Yes sir!"

Leaning very close, the pastor asked, "If you had two pigs, would you give Him one?"

"Cut that out, Pastor," the farmer snapped. "You know I have two pigs!"

The farmer talked like a generous giver, but when it came to translating principle into practice, it became clear that his heart was in the wrong place. This lack of generosity plagues the church today just as it did in the first century. The apostle Paul had to deal with people who were a lot like that farmer, and he wrote about the situation in his second letter to the church at Corinth.

The Corinthians were prosperous people. They were also proud of their biblical sophistication and boasted of their spirituality. So when Paul told them about an urgent need facing the church in Jerusalem, where the followers of Christ were being persecuted, the Corinthians made the largest financial pledge of all the churches Paul had contacted. But when the time came to collect the offering for the Jerusalem church, it was a different story.

Evidently the Corinthians were slow to complete their pledge, so Paul sent his fellow worker Titus back to Corinth with a letter written specifically to encourage them to finish what they had started. In 2 Corinthians, the apostle gently taught this prosperous church about the grace of giving. I will quote a few verses from Paul's letter below, but it's worth reading chapters 8 and 9 in depth.

In these two chapters Paul mentioned grace six times. He taught the Corinthians that those who have received much must give much—not as payment for their salvation, but as an expression of thankfulness to God. We could never begin to repay the debt of our salvation, and God does not require it of us. He delights, however, in receiving our thanks and is pleased when we express our appreciation through the grace of giving.

BIBLICAL LESSONS IN GIVING

Paul taught a lesson in generosity by using the much poorer church of Macedonia as a gentle rebuke for the self-serving attitude of the Corinthians. As we look at this passage, take note of three things. The first is that practicing the grace of giving honors God.

1. Giving Honors God

This is how Paul described the generous actions of the Macedonian Christians:

> And now, brothers, we want you to know about the grace that God has given the Macedonian churches. Out of the most severe trial, their overflowing joy and their extreme poverty welled up in rich generosity. For I testify that they gave as much as they were able, and even beyond their ability. Entirely on their own, they urgently pleaded with us for the privilege of sharing in this service to the saints.[7]

Severe trial? Extreme poverty? That doesn't sound like circumstances that produce a generous offering. In fact, it seems as if Paul did not even want to press the Macedonians to participate in this offering. But verse 4 says that "entirely on their own" they "pleaded" with Paul for the "privilege" of participating in the offering for the church at Jerusalem.

Paul was aware that the Macedonians had not just hit a little speed bump; they were suffering greatly—and part of their suffering was financial in nature. Yet in the midst of their own hardship, the Macedonians insisted on helping to alleviate the suffering of their fellow believers. Paul commended their actions as an example of the grace of giving.

When you are experiencing a time of feasting in your life and you give God the crumbs off your plate, that doesn't honor God. But when you're facing the possibility of famine and you make a sacrificial gift in spite of your circumstances, you are honoring God. And He will never forget that. When everything is falling apart and you give sacrificially, you are learning the grace of giving.

Jesus made the same point when He related the story of the widow's mite, dramatized at the beginning of this chapter. Widows lived in a precarious situation in Bible times. No social welfare system existed then, and widows who had no sons to provide for them often faced starvation. Jesus contrasted the sacrificial nature of the woman's gift with the self-serving amounts donated by wealthy templegoers who made a great show of giving. The widow gave just two coins, the smallest coins in circulation, which was the minimum gift acceptable to the temple treasury. Yet according to Jesus, she made the most generous gift of all.

The normal human reaction when we're going through trials is to ignore the suffering of others. We're tempted to think, "I can barely pay my own bills. I just can't help anybody else right now." Recalling the widow at the temple, however, we realize this is not the attitude of those who have freely received the grace of God. Grace-givers understand that problems are simply a part of life; we will always have them. Because of the grace of God, our own trials make us more sympathetic with other people's trials. Grace-givers become more sensitive to the pain of others, more understanding of their weaknesses, more patient with those who are struggling, more willing to help financially. Grace-givers allow their trials to move them to minister to others with compassion.

In 2 Corinthians we read that out of their most severe trial, the Macedonian Christians overflowed with joy, and they expressed that joy by giving. What could have made them joyful when they were facing severe trials? They took joy in the fact that God's grace had found them, that they had been brought out of the darkness of paganism into the light of Christ, and that they were on their way to spending eternity in heaven. The joy of their salvation overflowed into the joy of giving.

The grace of giving is never an obligation, like paying income taxes. If you view giving to God the same way you view paying taxes, then you are missing out on the overflowing joy that comes from being a "hilarious" giver—the literal translation of the phrase "cheerful giver" in 2 Corinthians 9:7. The word translated *cheerful* is the Greek word *hilaros,* which has the connotation not just of cheerfulness but of exuberance and merriment.

Grace giving is enjoyable. It is *hilarious* giving in the true sense of the word, and it is those who give with hilarity whom God loves.

Let me explain what I mean by hilarious giving. When Paul taught the Corinthians about the grace of giving, he used the analogy of planting and harvesting. He told them that if they sowed sparingly, they would reap sparingly, but if they sowed generously, they would reap generously.[8] Then he said, "Each man should give what he has decided in his heart to give, not reluctantly or under compulsion, for God loves a cheerful giver."[9]

The actual amount of our gifts may be quite small, but they can appear large in the eyes of God. As God measures our giving, a large gift is a gift of any amount—as long as it is given sacrificially. It's not the size of the gift that counts but the size of the heart that gives it. In addition, the sacrifice has to be made freely and willingly. Grace-givers learn to be hilarious givers, and in return they receive an outpouring of God's blessings.

2. Giving Invites God's Blessings

Severe trials and extreme poverty do not necessarily produce grace giving, even among Christians. Often, facing difficulty does the opposite. Trials and poverty can make people bitter and tight-fisted. In contrast, the grace giving exemplified by the Macedonian Christians was rooted in the secret for receiving God's blessing: They first gave of themselves, then of their substance.

In describing their offering Paul wrote, "And they did not do as we expected, but they gave themselves first to the Lord and then to us in keeping with God's will."[10] To be a Christian means only one thing: giving your life over to Christ. You trust Him with your most treasured possession—your soul. You commit to Him your eternal future.

The sad part is that some people are willing to commit their souls—but not their money—to Christ. Could it be that they prize money above their souls? If a person has that value system, could it be that he has not really given his life to Christ at all? Paul said the Macedonians "gave themselves first to the Lord." Everything else was just "things," never to be prized at the same level as giving oneself. Things are not of paramount importance for those who have experienced the grace of God in a life-changing way.

The grace of hilarious giving invites God's blessings. Second Corinthians promises this blessing: "God is able to make all grace abound to you, so that in all things at all times, having all that you need, you will abound in every good work.... You will be made rich in every way so that you can be generous on every occasion, and through us your generosity will result in thanksgiving to God."[11] When you follow the example of cheerful giving—hilarious giving—all your needs will be met, and you will have adequate resources to continue investing in God's work. That is God's promise to you.

3. Giving Is God's Model

Paul commended the Macedonian Christians for their generous gifts, but our standard for generous giving is far higher than the example set by the Macedonians. The grace giving of the Lord Jesus is the ultimate example. Paul expressed it this way: "For you know the grace of our Lord Jesus Christ, that though he was rich, yet for your sakes he became poor, so that you through his poverty might become rich."[12]

Jesus was born in a stable, and as an adult He had "no place to lay his head."[13] So why did Paul describe Jesus as being "rich"? Prior to the incarnation, everything in heaven and on earth belonged to Christ, but He voluntarily laid it all aside so that He could be born in poverty and die on the cross for our salvation. Never in the history of the universe did anyone abandon so much in order to become so poor that so many might become so rich in grace.

When you practice grace giving, you are following the model of Christ.

THE ULTIMATE CONTENTMENT

Living in grace and giving in grace go hand in hand. Those who have received much must give much—not as payment for salvation but as an expression of gratitude to God. Our trials should make us more sensitive and sympathetic to the suffering of others, and this understanding produces the ability to minister to others with compassion. That is a sign of God's grace at work in our lives.

In the early chapters of this book, we looked at the loss of contentment that can steal peace from our hearts and lead to destructive attempts to quiet the inner restlessness. We have also seen that true peace for our restless hearts comes only through God's grace. The highest experience of peace and contentment on earth is found in the life of obedience to God. The life of faith follows a path of spiritual restlessness right to God's heart. We enjoy the peace of God on earth as we live in His grace and respond in obedience with gratitude and generosity.

Still, earthly peace and contentment are but shadows of what is to come. A day looms in the future when God will judge the world so He can establish the heavenly Jerusalem where His children will enjoy the Lord's presence forever. God began human history in a paradise known as the Garden of Eden, where the first humans enjoyed complete, unhindered fellowship with God. Likewise, God will end earthly history with a garden city, a heavenly city known as the New Jerusalem. In that city, we will dwell with Him for eternity. And that, at long last, will put an end to our restless wandering, our longing for more, and our ongoing search for a place of rest and belonging. All of these will end when we are joined to God for eternity.

Let's turn the page and take a look at our final destination—our exciting, unparalleled, heavenly home.

Part 5

THE END OF DISCONTENTMENT

God has framed human history between two gardens—the earthly paradise of the Garden of Eden and the eternal joy of the garden city known as the New Jerusalem. The first is forever lost due to the sin of Adam and Eve. The second is yet to come, made possible by the sacrifice of Jesus Christ.

The New Jerusalem is the promised heavenly city where God will dwell forever with His children. As we conclude our look at divine discontent—that lack of peace that drives us until we are joined to God—let's get a preview of the new paradise that God is preparing for all believers.

Eleven

THE DIVINE END TO DISCONTENT

God's Promise of Peace and Rest Today and Forever

In our search for a solution to the loss of contentment that plagues humanity, we have seen that it's a spiritual journey. Forces in life attempt to push us in one of two directions. Some push us away from God as we pursue earthly solutions to our lack of peace. But in contrast to that wandering is the wooing of God's grace, which pushes us (or should I say, draws us) toward God. If we are open to God and honestly seeking Him, He eventually shows us that our home is with Him. God's grace brings contentment and puts an end to our wandering.

Scripture mirrors this journey, beginning in a search for earthly solutions and ending when we find our home in God. We began the human story in Genesis, in the garden paradise of Eden. The sin of the first humans broke their fellowship with God, and succeeding generations sought meaning and answers in the city of man. God continued to pursue His willful, rebellious people in love and mercy, first giving the nation of Israel an earthly city where God could be worshiped and glorified. Jerusalem was home to the temple, where God's people came to offer sacrifices and to worship the Lord. But God's people again rebelled and were carried off into captivity—far from the earthly City of God.

Again our God of grace pursued His willful people, sending His Son who submitted His life to the will of His Father. In a garden Jesus struggled with the cost of the sacrifice God was asking Him to make. Praying with such intensity that His sweat fell like great drops of blood, Jesus settled the matter, saying, "Yet not my will, but yours be done."[1] To pay the price for the sin and rebellion that began in the Garden of Eden, Jesus submitted His will in obedience to the Father while praying in the Garden of Gethsemane.

After submitting to God's will, Jesus laid down His life on a cross, on a hill called Golgotha. His ultimate sacrifice made possible the eternal rest we all seek. And now, two thousand years later, we look ahead to God's next provision for our ultimate contentment—the garden city of God.

In Revelation we read about the permanent dwelling place for everyone who has placed his faith in Christ throughout the millenniums. In this promised garden city, we will be fully restored to the intimate communion with God for which we were created. At long last our restless wandering will end in an eternity shared with God.

Ever since Adam and Eve were evicted from the Garden of Eden, humanity has been looking for a city. Cain and his descendants foolishly sought a home in the city of man. But their city was a place of rebellion, not a place of peace and rest. The heavenly city that God promises is the same place that Abraham, by faith, looked forward to, described in Scripture as "the city with foundations, whose architect and builder is God."[2] This city of God has foundations, which implies permanence, and for that reason we often refer to it as the eternal city.

The ancient city of Jerusalem foreshadowed "the city that is to come."[3] The Bible also refers to this future city as "the heavenly Jerusalem"[4] and "the Holy City, the new Jerusalem."[5] Earthly Jerusalem was considered a holy city because God allowed Solomon to build a "home" for Him there. From that time forward, the temple of Jerusalem became the focal point for worshiping God in the Hebrew faith. But as Christians, *we* have now become the temples of the Holy Spirit.[6] There is no longer a need for an earthly temple because the ultimate sacrifice for sin has been offered once and for all in Jesus.

The city of man still holds many allures, even for believers. In fact, there is so much that pulls our attention away from God that one of the greatest challenges for Christians today is how to reside in the city of man while dwelling spiritually in the city of God. Is it possible to enjoy the excitement and beauty of God's earthly creation without losing sight of our ultimate destination? How do we enjoy God's blessings and love this life while loving eternal life even more?

Few of us can echo the writer of Hebrews: "For here we do not have an enduring city, but we are looking for the city that is to come."[7] Sometimes we struggle so hard to keep the proper perspective between the earthly realm and the eternal that we lose an awareness of our heavenly future. We need to remind ourselves that even now "our citizenship is in heaven."[8] Heaven is not just a far-off vacation spot we will visit in the distant future. As believers in Christ, we are *already* citizens of heaven—and when you look at it that way, life on Planet Earth is nothing more than a short layover before we enter our heavenly home.

Since we already have our visas for the eternal city of God, let's consult our travel guide—the Bible—to learn more about our final destination. As I did with the Garden of Eden, I want to point out several characteristics of heaven, and they all start with the letter *p* to make them easier to remember.

Our Heavenly Home

More than six hundred verses in the Bible mention heaven, yet God's Word gives few details about the nature of His eternal city. I can only speculate that the reason Scripture is silent about the splendor of heaven is that we'd be looking for shortcuts to get there if we knew the full story!

Here are six important truths that we know about our heavenly home, the New Jerusalem.

1. It Is a Prepared City

Shortly before He died, Jesus told his disciples, "In my Father's house are many rooms; if it were not so, I would have told you. I am going there to prepare a place for you. And if I go and prepare a place for you, I will come back and take you to be with me that you also may be where I am."[9]

This statement was not intended solely for the original followers of Jesus. Every believer from every generation has a special room reserved in the heavenly city. What a privilege and honor that the Lord Jesus Christ Himself is preparing heaven for us! Scripture refers to the church, the entire body of believers past, present, and future, as the bride of Christ. Just as a bridegroom provides a home for his new bride, Jesus has returned to heaven to prepare a room for us so that we may dwell with Him in the Father's house forever.

2. It Is a Populated City

An untold number of angelic beings populate the New Jerusalem, constantly praising and serving God. Millions of believers inhabit that city right now, with millions more due to arrive. Jesus, the Lamb of God, resides at the center of its glory.[10] People often ask, "Who are we going to see in heaven?" The answer is all of the Old Testament saints, such as Abraham, who by faith looked forward to the coming of Christ, as well as all of the New Testament saints who by faith looked back to the Cross of Christ and trusted Him for their salvation. Beyond the saints we read about in Scripture will be all of the church, the entire family of God, past, present, and future.

3. It Is a Palatial City

How can you accurately describe a city whose characteristics surpass human thought and language? The best of what we have on earth is still only a dim reflection, a thin shadow of the awesomeness of heaven. Think of what excites you the most in life, then magnify that a billion times—and you still won't have a true picture of heaven.

The apostle Paul said that he knew a man who had been "caught up to the third heaven" and "heard inexpressible things, things that man is not permitted to tell."[11] The third heaven is the realm where God dwells. Scripture tells us that "God created the *heavens* [note the plural usage] and the earth."[12] And when He ascended to the Father, Jesus passed "through the *heavens.*"[13] The first heaven is what we would call the sky, the earth's atmosphere. The second heaven is outer space, the home of the stars and planets. To reach the third heaven requires traveling even farther, into the presence of God Himself.

The apostle John was an eyewitness to events transpiring in heaven, and the Holy Spirit instructed him to write down what he saw. John described thunderous praise accompanied by rapturous music. The unspeakable joy of seeing the Savior face to face will be transporting. The splendor of God's *shekinah* glory and the brilliance of the bright Morning Star—Jesus Himself—will be breathtaking. Again, mere words are inadequate to convey the indescribable qualities of the heavenly city.

4. It Is a Pleasant Place

Can you imagine a city where the crime rate is zero? where there is absolutely no conflict—not even a hint of tension or disharmony? Heaven is that place. It is a place of total peace, like no earthly peace we have ever experienced.

God has also promised that in His city there will be no suffering, no sickness, no death. Nor will there be any pain or anything that could cause people to weep. Why? Because God Himself "will wipe every tear from their eyes. There will be no more death or mourning or crying or pain, for the old order of things has passed away."[14]

Heaven is a place of reunion with our loved ones who have gone on before us. The sorrow and pain of separation will be obliterated, and we will never again remember our anguish.

5. It Is a Perfect Place

There will be no imperfection in heaven, since anything that would be incompatible with the holiness of God cannot exist there. We will face no temptation to sin, for the enemy of our souls will be banished to a lake of fire. As residents of heaven, we will be perfectly holy, just as the Lord Jesus Christ is holy.

No wonder writers often refer to both heaven and the Garden of Eden as *paradise.* I have been referring to the New Jerusalem as the "garden city" of God. Eden was merely an earthly reflection of the unparalleled beauty and perfection of God's dwelling place in the heavens.

While it is a place of tranquility and peace, heaven is not a place for idleness. To be sure, we will rest from the spiritual warfare that consumes us on earth. We will cease our struggles against the flesh, and our consciences will be free from the pangs of guilt and the torments of regret. But we will nevertheless be busy serving Jesus, ruling and reigning with Him.

6. It Is a Permanent Place

The book of Hebrews tells us that heaven is a country with permanent residents.[15] As we have seen, God is the chief architect and builder of heaven, and what He has constructed will endure for eternity. In the place Jesus has prepared for us, buildings will never collapse because of earthquakes or terrorist strikes.

One of the most inspirational pieces I've ever read about heaven is actually a letter written by an elderly man to Charles E. Fuller, an evangelist and radio pioneer who broadcast *The Old-Fashioned Revival Hour* from the 1930s to the late 1960s. I want to share an excerpt from that

letter because it was penned by someone who possessed a clear understanding of heaven and eternity.

> Next Sunday you are to talk about heaven. I am interested in that
> land because I have held a clear title to a bit of property there for
> over fifty years. I did not buy it; it was given to me without money
> and without price. But the donor purchased it for me at a tremen-
> dous sacrifice. I am not holding it for speculation since the title is
> not transferable.
>
> It is not a vacant lot. For more than a half-century I have
> been sending materials out of which the greatest architect and
> builder of the universe has been building a home for me which
> will suit me perfectly and will never have to be repaired. Ter-
> mites can never undermine its foundation for it rests upon the
> Rock of Ages. Fire cannot destroy it. Floods cannot wash it
> away. It is ready for me to enter in and abide in peace eternally
> without fear of being evicted.
>
> I hope to hear your sermon [on the radio] on Sunday next
> from my home here, but I have no assurance that I shall be able
> to do so. My ticket to heaven has no date stamped upon it, no
> return coupon, and no permit for baggage. I am ready to go,
> and I may not be here when you are talking next Sunday, but if
> not, I shall meet you there some day.[16]

Indeed, by the time Dr. Fuller received the letter, its author had journeyed to the eternal home that had been prepared for him. Each time I
read this letter, I am reminded that as believers we may be in this world
but we are not of it.[17] Our citizenship truly is in heaven.

Those who have received God's grace have been given a royal

commission as ambassadors of Christ. Our calling is to be salt for a rotting society, to be a light shining in the darkness of the city of man. Again and again Scripture reminds us not to get so comfortable in man's city that we lose sight of our eternal destination.

LOSING TOUCH WITH HOME

Why, then, are Christians apt to forget that ultimate contentment comes from God and that we will fully experience rest and peace in heaven, our true native country? I believe there are five reasons people become distracted by seeking contentment in the things of earth rather than the things of God.

1. A False Perception of the New Jerusalem

Most of us fail to stop and dwell on the magnificent glory of heaven. Unlike the man who wrote the letter to Dr. Fuller, most people think of heaven as a vague, ethereal place where we will sit around on clouds and play harps. Many think heaven is populated by the greeting-card version of angels—blond-haired, chubby-cheeked cherubs. As we have seen, that image bears no resemblance to the majesty and glory of the city that needs neither sun nor moon because God Himself is its light.[18]

2. The Overwhelming Pressures of Life

If we're not careful, the emotional wear and tear of life will steal our attention away from eternal matters. We can easily become mired in hurt, rejection, pain, and anger. Or we succumb to the pressures of juggling the responsibilities of a family, a home, a job, and our church involvement. Day-to-day irritations drain us mentally and sap our spiritual strength. Our frustration rises when we have to deal with stressed-out teachers and day-care workers, rude store clerks and forgetful waiters, ungrateful bosses, and insensitive friends. Financial responsibilities, relationship problems, health problems—all combine to eclipse our vision of the city of God.

The Lord wants us to be faithful even while we are facing the demanding responsibilities of life. He wants us to serve Him in all we do so that we can draw the attention of the world to the Savior. We must let people know that we live the way we do because we have a home in heaven and that they, too, may be forgiven by God and enjoy eternity in the New Jerusalem.

3. The Allure of What Is Seen

Because of human nature, whatever we see gets our immediate attention. We are captured by what's right in front of us, which prevents a focus on what is invisible. Heaven is "out of sight," therefore it remains "out of mind."

We tend to believe what is verifiable, and we prefer to verify it visually. Then we fall into the trap of believing that the life we can see will go on forever, so we invest everything we have in this life. Even the least money-oriented among us can be sucked into the materialism of this world. We make business and financial plans as if we were going to live forever. We give God nothing but leftovers. Somehow we don't stop long enough each day to ask what would happen to our plans if we went home to heaven this afternoon. Remember, you never know when you may be about to meet the Lord face to face.

4. The Worldliness of the Church

Walk into the average church and ask the members what their spiritual goals are. Ask how they are accomplishing the purpose for their existence. Some people will scratch their heads and say they hadn't given it that much thought. Some will shuffle their feet and stammer something about a committee that is working on a mission statement. And still others will whip out a full-blown marketing plan, complete with neighborhood maps and detailed objectives for developing a church that provides a welcoming and comfortable environment for those who are seeking God.

Contrast that with the church of the first century. Their number-one goal was to bring glory to the name of Jesus. Today many churches are ashamed to proclaim Him as the only way to heaven—even though the Lord Himself said, "I am the way and the truth and the life. No one comes to the Father except through me."[19]

Where the early church placed a high priority on holiness, today we have exchanged holiness for happiness. The early church measured success in terms of eternal gain, not church growth or prosperity. But today many people preach health and wealth here on earth. Why would they spend time thinking about heaven if they believe they can get everything they want right here?

5. A False Doctrine of Heaven and Hell

The majority of Americans think that when they die they will automatically go to heaven. In recent years Mormon-turned-New-Ager Betty Eadie popularized that position in her book *Embraced by the Light*. Others, like entertainer and author Shirley MacLaine, have long been touting a different view of eternity: They believe that reincarnation will take them from life to life to life.

What is truly alarming is that many mainline churches, and an ever-growing number of evangelicals, have advanced the universalist position, believing that God saves everyone. In their view, God's mercy would not allow Him to send anyone to a literal hell. Actually, this statement is both true and false. It is true because there *is* in fact a literal hell. But the statement is also false because *God* is never the One who sends anyone to hell. Those who end up in hell will send themselves there by refusing God's provision for their salvation. The Bible says that the Lord is "not willing that any should perish, but that all should come to repentance."[20] Hell is not what God desires for anyone, but those who reject His offer of salvation will experience eternal separation from Him—by their own choice.

Now, I know the question that arises in people's minds: "What about those who have never heard of Jesus Christ?" My answer to that is simple: Don't worry about those who have never heard the gospel. They are not your responsibility; they are God's responsibility. What you will be judged on is this: *You* heard the gospel of Jesus Christ—what did you do with it?

A few years ago a mainline minister sat across from me in my office. He looked me in the eyes and said, "How arrogant for you to think that Jesus is the only way to heaven!" I told him it wasn't my idea, that Jesus Himself is the One who stated this truth. None of my arguments persuaded him.

This man's attitude is typical of those who propagate false doctrines about heaven and hell. On June 26, 2000, three hundred people from more than thirty nations gathered at Carnegie Music Hall in Pittsburgh, Pennsylvania, to witness the signing of a charter for a new organization. The birth of the United Religions Initiative was the fulfillment of a vision that William Swing, an Episcopalian bishop from California, had nurtured since a 1995 interfaith service in San Francisco.

The stated purpose of the United Religions Initiative is not to create a one-world religion but to promote interfaith cooperation for peace and healing. "The URI is a bridge-building organization," the charter states, "not a religion."[21] The charter goes on to say, "We respect the sacred wisdom of each religion, spiritual expression, and indigenous tradition."[22] It seems clear that the URI believes that all faiths are created equal, and what one believes has no eternal consequence.

Today the URI has members from forty-seven nations, representing eighty-eight diverse religions, "spiritual expressions," and "indigenous traditions." Members are assured that they will not be proselytized,[23] so any expression of the belief that Jesus Christ is the only way to heaven would probably get you ejected from the organization.

NOT HOME YET

After forty years of ministry in Africa, missionary Henry C. Morrison retired. He sailed back to the United States, and after many days at sea the ship docked at a wharf in New York harbor. One particular passenger on board the ship was met with great fanfare: President Theodore Roosevelt, who was returning from a safari in Africa. Political pals and ardent admirers had gathered at the pier to catch a glimpse of the president, and the news media rushed to report the event.

Morrison felt dejected as he walked down the gangplank. A huge crowd had gathered to welcome the president home, but not a single person was there to greet the missionary and his wife. After four decades of faithful service overseas, this man was receiving no recognition at all.

Later, as he was traveling by train to his home in the Midwest, Morrison couldn't help expressing his disappointment to God. While he was praying, he sensed a small voice whispering in his ear, "But Henry, you're not home yet."[24]

God has planned a great homecoming for His children in the eternal city—a welcome-home party that will surpass anything we can imagine. I am eagerly looking forward to that day of celebration, for when I reach my heavenly home my soul will finally be at rest.

An End to Discontent

God has "set eternity in the hearts of men," Solomon told us.[25] Our nagging sense of inner restlessness can become the driving force to bring us into a personal relationship with God or bring us back to God if we have known Him but have wandered away. Because we are created by God and made in His image, something inside tells us there is more than what we see in the physical world, more than what we can comprehend through our rational minds.

We are pushed to the limit by the demands of modern life, leaving us weary and distraught. We are hounded by regret. We are worried and often filled with anxiety. Even those who don't recognize this dis-ease as a spiritual issue are familiar with the crying need for rest, peace, and security. Discontent is a spiritual issue that requires a spiritual solution, and God alone provides what we hunger for.

God's deliverance and care bring rest to the soul:

The LORD is gracious and righteous;
>   our God is full of compassion.
The LORD protects the simplehearted;
>   when I was in great need, he saved me.
Be at rest once more, O my soul,
>   for the LORD has been good to you.[26]

God intended rest to be a part of the natural rhythm of physical life. The Bible says that on the seventh day of Creation, the Sabbath day, the Lord rested from all His labor. He designed rest into the spiritual realm as well, holding out rest as the destination and satisfaction of our spiritual longing. Mankind's restless discontent is a search for the rest promised by the Lord, the rest that brings peace and repose to our troubled hearts. Only when our wandering leads us home to the Father will we find the peace and contentment we seek.

God continues to extend the invitation: "The promise of entering his rest still stands…. There remains, then, a Sabbath-rest for the people of God."[27] My prayer is that you will accept God's invitation and enter into the rest that only He can offer—starting in this life and continuing for eternity in the life to come.

Finding Contentment
in the God of Grace

Chapter 1: The Root of Discontentment

1. What things or circumstances steal your contentment? What are some of the ways you have dealt with feelings of discontent?

2. Which biblical event planted the root of all dissatisfaction in humanity?

3. Why do you think Adam and Eve risked losing the paradise of the Garden of Eden when they first entertained the thought of disobeying God?

4. After they were cast out of the garden, how did Adam and Eve's life change?

5. Did God's love for Adam and Eve change as a result of their sin? Does God's love for you change when you seek satisfaction in things that are not of Him?

Chapter 2: Building a Place to Hide

1. What emotion fueled Cain's murderous rage against his brother? In what ways do you see this same dynamic fueling violence in the world today?

2. Cain became a wanderer, settling in a region east of Eden. Can you identify with the feeling of being a "restless wanderer"? Which life circumstances create the most restlessness in your soul?

3. God often calls us to come closer to Him so that He may reveal sin in our lives. He wants to remove our sin and guilt. Has God been calling you closer to Him? If so, what is He telling you?

4. What do the four characteristics of the city of man teach us about the futility of creating distance between ourselves and God?

5. When was the last time you recognized one of the four characteristics in your own life? What did you do to address the harmful effects?

Chapter 3: Competing with God

1. Can you remember the last time you set out to accomplish something without consulting God or asking for His guidance and help? What was the outcome of that venture?

2. There is a renewed fascination with pagan religion and occult practices in our culture. What evidence have you seen of the "Babylonian revival"?

3. Do you have a strong interest in the zodiac, or have you ever consulted a psychic or other fortune-teller? If so, do you see how those practices run counter to God's desire to guide your life?

4. In ancient Babylon the people banded together to build a tower designed for the worship of stars and false gods. What did God do to prevent the completion of the construction project?

5. As you approach your daily responsibilities, in what area do you most need to trust God for provision, protection, or direction?

Chapter 4: From Desperation to Hope

1. The world situation and our individual lives are so unsettled that it would be easy to sink into despair. What aspect of life is causing you the most concern right now?

2. David's son Absalom rallied support in Israel for a palace coup. As David left Jerusalem to take up a position outside the city, how did he express his anguish to God?

3. Can you identify with David's thirst for God, which the king expressed as he waited on further word about his son's murderous plans?

4. How did David find encouragement in the midst of his depression?

5. The Bible tells us that our ultimate hope is found in Jesus Christ. What does having this hope mean to you?

Chapter 5: The Pursuit of Peace

1. God sometimes stirs restlessness in a person in order to move her to a place where she can be used to further God's purposes. Can you identify on some level with the obedient wandering of Abraham, Ruth, or Joseph? If so, what was the outcome of your wandering?

2. We also see in Scripture that people have wandered because of ingratitude, pride, or rebellion. How do you determine the difference between a selfish lack of contentment and the restlessness that comes from God?

3. God sent Abraham on a sojourn simply by telling him to leave his home and promising that eventually He would reveal a destination. How do you think you would respond to such a command from the Lord?

4. Jesus Christ left heaven so He could pay the penalty for our sins. To fulfill God's purpose, He left His home to sojourn on earth. Have you placed your trust in Jesus' sacrifice for your sins?

5. Most of the people in Jesus' day rejected Him as the promised Messiah. How did He react when the people of Jerusalem refused to believe in Him?

Chapter 6: Coming Home to the God of Grace

1. The parable of the prodigal son begins with an ungrateful young man leaving home—choosing earthly pleasure over nearness to his father. Has there been a time in your life when you were running from God? If so, what made you run?

2. The story continues with the young man—penniless and humiliated in a faraway land—realizing that he had turned his back on his father's love. The prodigal son decides to return home, wondering if his father will accept him or send him away. What strikes you most about the father's reaction to his son's return?

3. The Bible teaches that God takes the initiative in reaching out to us to save us and to draw us to Himself. How does the free gift of God's grace differ from the core teachings of other religions?

4. God has shown Himself to be a God of grace from the beginning. How did He demonstrate His grace to Adam and Eve?

5. Human nature tells us that we have to work hard to be "good enough" to enter heaven. Can anyone enter heaven based on his or her own merits?

Chapter 7: Confronting Our Weaknesses

1. As humans we are finite and flawed, vulnerable to weakness. What would you say are the primary areas of weakness in your life?

2. God said to Paul, "My power is made perfect in weakness" (2 Corinthians 12:9). Such a statement defies human logic but makes sense on a spiritual level. What does it mean to you?

3. Paul asked God three times to remove the "thorn in the flesh" that tormented him. Based on God's response to Paul's request (see above), do you believe thorns, or times of suffering, always result from our sin?

2. God stands in opposition to the proud but gives His grace to those who are humble (see James 4:6, which echoes Proverbs 3:34). In what ways does prayer help to defeat our pride and make us humble?

3. Most Christians struggle with prayer for a variety of reasons. What obstacles to prayer do you encounter most frequently?

4. God invites us to approach His throne of grace "with confidence" (see Hebrews 4:16). Is there ever a reason for a Christian to be timid about going to God in prayer?

5. During prayer, it is sometimes difficult to put into words just what we are feeling or what it is that we need. At other times we're unsure how we should pray about a particular situation. When we're struggling in prayer, how does God come to our rescue? (See Romans 8:26-27.)

Chapter 10: Cheating Ourselves Out of Blessing

1. Jesus commended the widow's meager offering because she gave it out of her poverty. Can you think of things you have done without in order to give financially to support the work of God's kingdom?

2. We live in the wealthiest nation on earth, yet most Christians in America give only a tiny percentage of their income to God. Why do you think it is so difficult for some Christians to give to the Lord?

3. The Christians in Macedonia were suffering tremendous trials when they gave their offering to assist Christians in Jerusalem. What was their approach to God that made it easier for them to give generously in spite of their poverty? (See 2 Corinthians 8:5.)

4. God is seeking not those who give out of obligation but those who find great joy in giving. What blessings accompany cheerful giving? (See 2 Corinthians 9:6-11.)

4. When we are faced with adversity, our first impulse is to solve the problem using our own resources—our intellect, our problem-solving skills, our willingness to work hard to find a solution. How does this human impulse compare to God's promise of grace to meet every need that we have, including our needs during times of suffering?

5. Think back to times in your life when you depended on God the most. Do those times of trusting God correspond with times of ease or times of difficulty?

Chapter 8: The Lie of Legalism

1. Which religious leaders in Jesus' day were the foremost practitioners of legalism? What evidences of legalism do you see today in Christian circles?

2. Legalism adds man-made rules to God's requirements found in Scripture. Can you identify any legalistic practices or beliefs in your own life?

3. If grace is the free and unmerited favor of God, in what way is legalism the opposite of grace?

4. In his letter to the Christians in Galatia, Paul linked legalism to the idea of falling from grace (see Galatians 5:4). If a person has truly accepted Jesus Christ as his Lord and Savior, is there anything he can do to "fall from grace"?

5. Is there anything that keeps you from trusting fully in God's free gift of grace? If so, ask God to enable you to rely completely on Him and to let go of any tendency to try to "earn" His favor.

Chapter 9: The Pitfall of Pride

1. Because of our inherited sin nature, pride comes naturally to each of us. But its consequences are always destructive. In what ways do you struggle most with pride?

5. Do you sometimes find yourself giving out of a sense of duty rather than out of joy? If so, what can you do this week to become a more cheerful giver?

Chapter 11: The Divine End to Discontent

1. As we draw near to God, we begin to experience inner peace and contentment on earth. Can you think of specific ways that God has already met your longing for contentment?

2. Scripture teaches that Christians are citizens of heaven even while living on earth (see Philippians 3:20; Ephesians 2:6). How has reading chapter 11 changed your understanding of heaven?

3. Jesus returned to heaven to prepare a place where His followers will spend eternity, yet most Christians spend very little time thinking about heaven. From chapter 11, what are five things that distract Christians from pondering the glories of heaven?

4. The angels of heaven spend their days praising and worshiping the Lord (see Revelation 5:11-14). When we praise God on earth, our voices are joined with the voices of heaven. Join the heavenly chorus right at this moment by singing a song of praise to our Lord.

5. It is possible to be certain of your salvation. If you are questioning whether you have been forgiven of your sins, turn to Appendix A and pray the Prayer to Receive Eternal Security Through Jesus Christ.

A Prayer to Receive Eternal Security Through Jesus Christ

Oh God, how great You are to love a sinner like me! I know that my inherited sin nature, in addition to the sins that I practice, will lead me to eternal judgment. I cannot save myself. I accept Jesus' payment on the cross for the wages of my sin. Forgive me of my sin. I repent of all my wrongdoing. Receive me now as Your child. Thank You that the Holy Spirit brought me to the point where I realize my need for You. Now I invite Him to dwell in me and to guide me as I read Your Word.

A Prayer to Renew Your Commitment to Jesus Christ

Father, thank You for the hope and strength available to me through Your Son, Jesus Christ. I confess that in my restlessness and discontent, I have sought answers apart from Your grace and Your unending love for me. I ask You now to renew my faith in the resurrected Lord Jesus. Pour Your Holy Spirit upon me in such a way that Jesus will become and always remain the primary focus in every area of my life. Forgive me of my unbelief, my wandering, and my sin. I thank You for answering my prayer because You have promised to hear those who come to You in humility and brokenness. I pray this in Jesus' name. Amen.

NOTES

Introduction

1. Augustine, *Confessions* (Oxford University Press, 1998), Book I, 1.
2. Kenneth W. Osbeck, *101 Hymn Stories* (Grand Rapids, Mich.: Kregel, 1982), 52.

Chapter 1

1. See Genesis 3:17-18.
2. Genesis 3:16.
3. Genesis 4:1.
4. Our word *paradise* comes from a Persian word that refers to a garden or enclosed park. The same word also connotes a place of peace and protection—exactly what the Garden of Eden was designed to provide.
5. Genesis 2:15.
6. Genesis 2:16-17.

Chapter 2

1. The Bible does not tell us anything about Cain's wife, but it's obvious that Cain married either his sister or a niece. That shocks a lot of people, but who else would there be for the first human beings to marry except their blood relatives? When God gave the Law to Moses, this practice changed, and marriage with close blood relatives was prohibited.
2. Genesis 4:10.
3. Genesis 4:9.
4. Genesis 4:4-5.
5. Genesis 4:12.
6. Genesis 4:17.

7. See Genesis 3:21.

8. See Genesis 4:19.

9. See Jeffrey P. Kahn, *Beauty by the Dozen?* Found at www.cnn.com/ HEALTH/9911/01/ethics.matters.

10. Genesis 4:23-24.

11. Genesis 6:5-7.

12. Genesis 6:8.

Chapter 3

1. The word *ziggurat* comes from the Akkadian word *ziqqurratu,* referring to an ancient Mesopotamian temple tower consisting of a lofty pyramidal structure built in successive stages with outside staircases and a shrine at the top.

2. See Genesis 10:8-12 and 11:1-9.

3. Genesis 9:25.

4. See Genesis 10:8.

5. See Genesis 4:16.

6. See Genesis 11:7-9.

7. Genesis 11:4.

8. See, for example, Deuteronomy 18:9-13; Leviticus 19:31; and Isaiah 48:13-14.

9. Found at http://nces.ed.gov/timss/results.asp.

10. Dinesh D'Souza, "Education's Self-esteem Hoax," *Christian Science Monitor,* 24 October 2002. Found at www.csmonitor.com/2002/1024/ p09s01-coop.html.

Chapter 4

1. See 2 Samuel 15:25-26.

2. See 2 Samuel 15:28.

3. See 2 Samuel 15:33-35.

4. See 2 Samuel 16:5-8.

5. 2 Samuel 12:10.

6. See Psalm 42:9.

7. Psalm 42:1-2. *The New International Version* labels this psalm as follows: "For the director of music. A *maskil* of the Sons of Korah." I believe the original language used here means that this psalm was *for* the sons of Korah, not that it was composed by them. I believe Psalm 42 to be a psalm of David.

8. See Prentiss Price, "All About Depression," found at www.allaboutdepression.com.

9. 1 Kings 19:4.

10. Jeremiah 20:14-18.

11. Psalm 42:1.

12. Jesus said, "Blessed are those who hunger and thirst for righteousness, for they will be filled" (Matthew 5:6).

13. Psalm 42:2.

14. Matthew 5:4.

15. Psalm 30:5.

16. Psalm 42:5-6.

17. 1 Samuel 30:6, KJV.

18. You can read the entire story in 1 Samuel 30:1-20.

19. Psalm 42:7.

20. Psalm 42:8.

21. Job 35:10.

22. Psalm 42:9.

23. Matthew 27:42-43.

24. Matthew 27:44.

25. Psalm 42:11.

26. Letter written January 23, 1841, to John T. Stuart, Abraham Lincoln's first law partner. Quoted in Roger Norton, *Depressed? Read Abraham Lincoln's Words,* Abraham Lincoln Research Site, http://home.att.net/~rjnorton/Lincoln84.html.
27. Norton, *Depressed?*
28. Romans 5:2-5.

Chapter 5

1. See 1 Samuel 17:45-47.
2. 1 Kings 8:15-18,20.
3. See Genesis 37:12-36.
4. See Genesis 43 and 46:1-5.
5. Genesis 45:5 and 50:20.
6. Ruth 1:16-17.
7. See Matthew 1:5-16 and Ruth 4:16-22.
8. Genesis 12:1.
9. See Genesis 17:5.
10. See Psalm 110:4; Hebrews 5:6-10; and 7:1-10.
11. See 2 Samuel 12:1-13 and Psalm 51.
12. Psalm 51:10-11.
13. See 2 Chronicles 7:1-3.
14. See Matthew 21:12-13.
15. Luke 19:41-44.
16. See Ezekiel 48:35.

Chapter 6

1. Luke 15:21.
2. See Luke 15:23.
3. Matthew 5:45.
4. See Genesis 2:16-17.

5. See Genesis 3:4.

6. See Genesis 3:14-15, the first mention in Scripture of the promised Messiah.

7. See Genesis 3:21.

8. Ephesians 2:1-2.

9. Ephesians 2:4-6.

10. See Ephesians 2:6.

11. Ephesians 2:8-9.

12. See Ephesians 2:10.

13. Ephesians 2:7.

Chapter 7

1. 2 Corinthians 12:9, NKJV.

2. 2 Corinthians 12:7-10.

3. See 1 Corinthians 2:1.

4. Galatians 6:11.

5. 2 Corinthians 11:24-28.

6. Found at www.christianitytoday.com/ct/2002/132/53.0.html.

7. 2 Corinthians 12:7.

8. Job 1:22.

Chapter 8

1. This statement was made in the presence of the author.

2. John 6:37-39.

3. Philippians 1:6.

4. Jude 24.

5. Galatians 5:4.

6. Galatians 3:1,3.

7. Galatians 5:13-14.

8. See Exodus 20:17 and Matthew 5:42.

9. Ephesians 1:6.

10. See Ephesians 1:8.

11. Galatians 5:1.

Chapter 9

1. Esther 4:13-14.

2. See Esther 4:16.

3. Esther 5:5.

4. Hebrews 4:14-16.

5. Revelation 20:11-12.

6. Revelation 20:15.

7. Matthew 7:9-11.

8. Romans 8:26.

9. John 14:16.

10. God serves us during times when we need consolation. Paul described God as "the Father of compassion and the God of all comfort, who comforts us in all our troubles, so that we can comfort those in any trouble with the comfort we ourselves have received from God" (2 Corinthians 1:3-4).

11. Hebrews 4:16.

12. Hebrews 10:11-12.

13. James 4:2-3.

14. Hebrews 10:19,22-24.

Chapter 10

1. Mark 12:17.

2. See Luke 20:46-47.

3. See Luke 21:3-4.

4. James B. Simpson, comp., *Simpson's Contemporary Quotations* (Boston: Houghton Mifflin, 1988), no. 3007.

5. Online NewsHour transcript from PBS's *Jim Lehrer's NewsHour,* "The Second Presidential Debate," 11 October 2000, found at www.pbs.org/newshour/bb/election/2000debates/2ndebate5.

6. Matthew 6:21, author's paraphrase.

7. 2 Corinthians 8:1-4.

8. See 2 Corinthians 9:6.

9. 2 Corinthians 9:7.

10. 2 Corinthians 8:5.

11. 2 Corinthians 9:8,11.

12. 2 Corinthians 8:9.

13. Luke 9:58.

Chapter 11

1. Luke 22:42.

2. Hebrews 11:10.

3. Hebrews 13:14.

4. Hebrews 12:22.

5. Revelation 21:2.

6. See 1 Corinthians 6:19.

7. Hebrews 13:14.

8. Philippians 3:20.

9. John 14:2-3.

10. See Revelation 21:23.

11. 2 Corinthians 12:2,4.

12. Genesis 1:1.

13. Hebrews 4:14.

14. Revelation 21:4.

15. See Hebrews 11:13-16.

16. Found at www.brentcards.net/email/greets39.shtml.

17. See John 17:15-16.

18. See Revelation 21:23.

19. John 14:6.

20. 2 Peter 3:9, KJV.

21. Principle #1, URI Charter, adopted 26 June 2000, found at www.uri.org/abouturi/charter.

22. Principle #2, URI Charter.

23. Principle #21, URI Charter.

24. Found at www.lhcf.org/sermons/010422.htm.

25. Ecclesiastes 3:11.

26. Psalm 116:5-7.

27. Hebrews 4:1,9.